Managing Yourself
Creatively

Managing Creatively
a Very Practical Guide in Two Volumes

Volume 1

Managing Yourself Creatively

by Ted Pollock, Ph.D.

Illustrations by
Ray Lewis

HAWTHORN BOOKS, INC.
Publishers / NEW YORK

To

who have managed together beautifully for almost sixty years

Contents

Introduction

Another book on management?

Not quite.

Two more books.* And without apology, although one visit to any large book store is all that is necessary to establish that there are more books—good, bad and worse—on the subject than any sane executive would ever willingly inflict upon himself. According to the most recent edition of the *Subject Guide to Books in Print,* there are some 400 books on management in print today. They range in scope from no-nonsense introductions to computer programming management to semihysterical outpourings on how to tap the hidden powers of your mind and make a million dollars, after taxes. Some proclaim management a science; others, an art. All, by virtue of being in print, tacitly claim that they are worth reading. So do these two.

What may make these two books somewhat different—and, consequently, commend them to your attention in an offbeat way—is that they are neither the end result of a nationwide survey of business leaders nor the distilled experience of fifty years of personal involvement with a major corporation, where I worked myself up from the mail room to the chairmanship of the board.

* This is the first of two companion volumes. The second is titled *Managing Others Creatively.*

No. These books rest on a firm foundation of four highly personal convictions or, perhaps, prejudices.

The first is that none of us lives up to his full potential all of the time. Yet, if we could improve our own performance—and the performances of those under us—by, say, a modest 10 percent on the average, we would be doing ourselves, our companies, and the economy itself an enormous amount of good. This is a worthwhile and realizable goal, one which I honestly believe these volumes can help most managers reach.

The second is that, aside from human life itself, there is nothing so precious as a good idea—and I have tried to unearth and cram as many good ideas as possible into these books.

The third is that no matter what anybody says, the successful management of oneself and others is nothing more—or less—than applied common sense which, as everyone concedes (firmly convinced that he is among the chosen), is not very common at all. I hope that nothing of what follows violates reason.

The fourth is that, regardless of the sophistication of our machinery, the subtlety of our planning or the modernity of our plants and laboratories, it is still, and always will be, *people* who make our companies go. The need for men and women who can manage others effectively, therefore, will only increase, not diminish. The emphasis in these books, consequently, is on the human element.

I should like to thank Bob Lincicome, Editor of *Electric Light & Power*, for inviting me to write these books. My admiration for his good judgment grows daily.

Finally, it would be remiss indeed not to acknowledge the continued encouragement of my wife, Barbara, who periodically whispered those three little words designed to sustain the most flagging of spirits and motivate the most chronic of procrastinators: "Get to work!"

Two more books on management—herewith.

Managing Yourself
Creatively

Chapter One

101 Questions
for Every Executive

Before you know how far you have to go on a journey, you must know where you are starting from. On that assumption, here is an exhaustive questionnaire which touches upon just about every aspect of management covered in these two volumes.

Read the following questions carefully and answer each as thoughtfully as you can. While many of them can be answered by a simple yes or no, others will take a lot more time.

There is no scoring system, no "average," no prize in the accepted sense. But there is a whopping personal reward for taking the test: an insight into your strengths and weaknesses as a manager. As those weaknesses emerge, note them well, for they will tell you to which of the following chapters you ought to devote the most time and attention. The result should be improved performance all around.

Since no one but yourself need ever see your answers, be as candid with yourself as possible. Got a pencil and paper? Get ready. Go!

1. Do you know how much one hour of your time is worth?

2. When was the last time you were at your desk before 9 A.M.? After 5 P.M.?

3. Is your day's schedule of activities firmly in your mind when you arrive at your office?

1

4. Do you have a fairly accurate idea of what you ought to get done this week? This month? This quarter?

5. Do you habitually find yourself taking work home at night and over weekends in order to "catch up"?

6. Honestly now, have you delegated as much work as possible to subordinates?

7. If, for some reason, you had to stay home for several days, would your more routine chores get done? By whom?

8. Do you use the telephone as a tool for getting things done with dispatch? Or do you often let it become a time-devourer?

9. Are you time conscious? For example, do you weigh accurately the time requirements of various tasks before assigning them to others or undertaking them yourself?

10. Do you tend to devote too much time to the things you like to do and too little to the less pleasant, but equally important, jobs?

11. Do you carry a notebook with you for jotting down ideas, important information, sudden insights, and so on, rather than rely on your memory?

12. Do you answer all letters, telephone calls, and memoranda promptly?

13. Does paper work take up an inordinate amount of your working day?

14. Is there a steady flow of communications between you and your people, with a minimum of backtracking, questions, and requests for clarification?

15. Do you use "stock paragraphs" to cover stock situations in your letters, thus saving time?

16. Do you make sure your instructions are clear and not ambiguous in any way before issuing them?

17. Do you subscribe to an "open-door" policy to encourage subordinates to drop by when there is something bothering them?

18. Is your secretary briefed on whom you will see, to whom you will speak on the telephone, and who should be handled by her?

19. Are your people conversant with such things as general company policy on pay, conditions of employment, vacations, sick pay, and other fringe benefits? Do they know their company's background, how it is making out, where it is going, what new products it is developing, and what improvements in its operation are in the offing?

20. Do you use periodic group meetings or individual conferences with employees to keep the channels of communication open (i.e., to air complaints, make announcements, issue instructions, pass along information)?

21. Are exceptional contributions by employees in your department or company recognized and rewarded?

22. Do you keep your instructions positive?

23. Are you ever guilty of using "gobbledygook" in your communications, either oral or written?

24. Is the top of your desk kept reasonably clear of accumulated work?

25. Do your people know where they fall short? What they can do to improve? What they are doing exceptionally well?

26. Do subordinates know that the "boss" has a real interest in them? That he is anxious for them to progress? That he will justly reward them for well-done jobs?

27. Do your people know what they are supposed to do at all times? What authority they have? What their business relationships are with other people in the company?

28. Can you truthfully say that the people under you have a sense of the importance of their work?

29. Are your subordinates kept informed on matters affecting them?

30. Do you keep your fingers on every little detail of the work done under you? Or do you hand out assignments and let subordinates take it from there, reporting progress—but not minutiae—to you?

31. Do you usually make your wishes known to those un-

der you via suggestions rather than orders and commands?

32. Do you make a conscientious effort to set a good example for your subordinates (e.g., by being punctual, meeting deadlines, showing enthusiasm for the job at hand, respect for others' opinions, and the like)?

33. A junior member of your staff approaches you with a bright, workable idea for saving money in your area of responsibility. Will he get full credit for his brainstorm? Will you help him work out any bugs in his idea?

34. Similarly, a subordinate comes to you with what he thinks is a good idea, but one which you know won't work. How do you let him down without discouraging him from approaching you in the future with other ideas?

35. Do you secure a lasting personal satisfaction from the success and development of your subordinates? Do you believe that growth in the people under you increases your own stature as an executive?

36. Name three of the people under you and describe the "hot button" of each. That is, what is the best way to motivate each one (e.g., appealing to his pride, sense of competition, ambition, desire to excel, and so on)?

37. Generally speaking, how would you describe the morale of the people who work under you?

38. Name the man best suited to step into your shoes in the event of your own promotion or retirement.

39. What have you been doing to make him even more capable?

40. Do you exchange ideas with your fellow executives aside from formal conferences and meetings?

41. Do you think your fellow executives consider you an authority in your field?

42. What has been the single biggest development in your field within the last five years?

43. What is the single biggest development in your field likely to be within the next five years?

44. Are you a good listener? That is, do people tend to "open up" to you?

45. Does your company subscribe to any special code of ethics? Describe it.

46. To what associations or other business organizations does your company belong?

47. As a result of its memberships, what benefits does your company enjoy?

48. Have you ever questioned a company policy or regulation—or do you accept on faith that, "They must know what they're doing"?

49. Are you a good-will ambassador for your company? In your official capacity, for example, do you belong to any civic organization, make speeches, serve on committees, etc.?

50. If applicable, name the agency that handles your firm's advertising.

51. Who is in charge of finance in your company? Engineering? Research and development? Operations? Personnel? Public relations?

52. Do you have at least a fair working knowledge of what each of the other departments in your firm does?

53. Are you a decisive person? Or do you constantly change your mind, worry about decisions already made, find yourself countermanding instructions previously issued?

54. Before attempting to reach a decision, do you try to assemble all the pertinent facts in a given situation?

55. Do you approach the decision-making process without preconceived notions, prejudices, assumptions, hopes, fears, and so forth?

56. Do you attempt to draw on the experience and wisdom of others before reaching a decision?

57. Do you ever use a pencil and paper as decision-making aids (e.g., for listing alternatives open to you, jotting down the pros and cons of a specific course of action, "turning over" your problem)?

58. Do you confront decision-making squarely? Or do you

postpone it as long as possible in the hope that it will somehow take care of itself?

59. Offhand, what would you say is your decision-making batting average?

60. Do you willingly accept the responsibility for your decisions?

61. When a setback occurs, do you try to analyze its causes and seek ways to prevent it from recurring?

62. If the setback is your own fault, do you face that fact and see what you can learn from it or do you seek refuge in rationalizations or other face-saving devices?

63. Are you ever guilty of taking out these setbacks on others through humiliating or shouting at them?

64. Can you shrug off a temporary defeat after a reasonable length of time—even see some humor in it—or do you sulk, lose your appetite, and make those around you uncomfortable?

65. Are you irritated when you run into opposition from a higher executive? Or do you honestly try to see the merit in his argument and, perhaps, learn something?

66. Are you concerned about getting credit for plans which you conceived?

67. Do you shelve a plan when you run into an unforeseen obstacle or do you try a) to remove the obstacle or b) to modify your plan so that the obstacle no longer exists?

68. When criticizing others, do you try to keep your remarks positive?

69. Do you avoid saying, or intimating, "*You* are to blame" and, instead, point out *what* was done wrong?

70. Do you remain calm while delivering a critique of another's performance?

71. When something goes wrong, do you *assume* who is to blame? Or do you objectively and conscientiously seek out the facts?

72. Have you ever used ridicule or sarcasm as methods of criticism?

73. Do you give your criticism in private? Praise in public?

74. Does your criticism usually work? Do those in error learn from you and mend their ways?

75. Can you take it as well as give it? When on the receiving end of criticism, do you view the experience as an opportunity to improve and learn? Or as a bitter pill to be swallowed quickly and forgotten?

76. Are you ever guilty of "I'm-beyond-criticism" thinking?

77. Can subordinates offer criticisms of you or your department? Or are they instructed, implicitly or explicitly, to keep their thoughts to themselves?

78. Can you recall any specific experiences in which you changed your way of doing something as a result of some personal criticism you received?

79. When was the last time you read a book on the techniques of management?

80. When was the last time you had a complete physical examination?

81. What would you say is your weakest point as an executive?

82. What have you done within the last thirty days to correct it?

83. Are you a brain-picker? Do you consciously and deliberately try to learn whatever you can from the people with whom you come into contact, be they your superiors, subordinates, or peers?

84. If you had to sum up the image of yourself carried around by your people, how would you describe it (e.g., a good leader, tough but fair, prejudiced, incompetent, erratic, etc.)?

85. Are you generally tactful? Can you get people to change their ways or do things without hurting their feelings?

86. When absolutely necessary, however, can you insist on an unpopular (but, to you, correct) course of action?

87. Do you have a hobby or outside interest that permits you to "get away from it all" occasionally and refresh your thinking as well as yourself?

88. Do you get some exercise every week?

89. When was the last time you admitted that you were wrong and changed your mind about—or attitude toward—a new idea, method, or person?

90. Where in your firm would you like to be a year from now? Five years? Ten years?

91. Specifically, what are you doing *now* to make those dreams come true?

92. If you had to describe your unique value to your firm in one short paragraph, what would you say?

93. What other executive in your firm do you envy for his ability? Why? How can you personally improve by emulating him?

94. When you have an idea that you consider good, but one with which others disagree, do you fight for it?

95. Your boss is following a course of action that you consider disastrous. Would you tell him so in no uncertain terms? Offer your critique in the form of a suggestion? Consider it none of your business?

96. You and another executive are up for promotion. The other man gets it. Would you *sincerely* congratulate him? Hate his guts, but hide your feelings? Hate his guts and make no attempt to disguise your attitude?

97. You have a rare opportunity to pull off a coup on behalf of your company (and, of course, yourself) that, while not illegal, would require you to wink at generally accepted ethical behavior. It's ten to one that no one but yourself will ever know. Would you follow through?

98. Regardless of your answer to the above question, explain why.

99. Do you ever throw out the "rule book" if you see a better way to achieve your goal?

100. If it were up to you, what would be changed in your firm?

101. To whose attention can you bring this idea—tactfully?

No matter what your answers were, you now have, perhaps for the first time, a fairly accurate idea of how you stack up as an executive. At this point, it shouldn't be difficult to recognize which of the following chapters you ought to read with special attentiveness. Why not make a point of returning to this questionnaire and taking it again in two or three months, after you have had an opportunity to put into practice some of the techniques described in the following pages? That way, you'll be able to chart your progress.

Heck! You may even surprise yourself!

Chapter Two

Twenty-Four Ways to Save Time

Even if you have a comfortable bank account and promptly meet all your financial obligations—you're probably a spendthrift!

Don't believe it?

Have you ever dawdled just a little longer in bed before getting up? Taken an extra coffee break? Knocked off early from work? Caught yourself watching a TV show you weren't even enjoying? Been appalled at how little of the week's work you've done by Friday afternoon? Wondered why you never have enough time to do the things you want to do?

If any of these questions hit home, you are a spendthrift with your time. Such squandering is even costlier than money-wasting, for if you have enough time, you can always earn money. But all the money in the world can't buy you one precious minute.

If, like most of us, you are tired of watching your days glide by with less solid achievement in them than you know you are capable of; if you want to stop "getting into debt to yesterday"; if you are sincerely interested in *making* more time for yourself—you can!

Getting more done in less time requires just two things: *organization* and *self-discipline*. Learn to make every minute count and rid yourself of the time-devouring habits many of us

unwittingly acquire over the years and you have gone a long
way toward stretching the time at your disposal.

Here are twenty-four specific ways to do just that.

1. PINPOINT YOUR GOAL

A lot of managers waste time and energy on a job simply
because they lack a clear idea of what they should do. Unable
to see where they're going, they make false starts, lose their
way, get discouraged, turn in performances unworthy of them.

Know your destination from the beginning, though, and
you'll get there a lot faster. Ask yourself, therefore, "What, precisely, do I want to accomplish?" Maybe you have to write a
report; revamp your budget; visit a customer; draw up an
agenda. Whatever it is, get it clear in your own mind. That's
crucial.

2. GET AN EARLY START

By rising just fifteen to twenty minutes earlier than you
do, you can get a jump on your whole day. More and more
executives are getting to their offices before the staff arrives so
that they can plan their day, jot down memos and get the ball
rolling in the pre-9 A.M. calm.

3. ANTICIPATE YOUR NEEDS

You can avoid the minor—but time-wasting—frustrations
that whittle away at our days by anticipating "little" crises.
That means having on hand an adequate supply of such everyday necessities as small change, tokens, stamps, paper clips,
stationery and so on. If necessary, have duplicates of keys,
shoelaces, eyeglasses, umbrellas, razor blades. Decide at night
what you will wear the next day. A five- or ten-dollar bill
tucked away in your wallet can often "save the day." (But don't
forget your wallet!)

4. CONCENTRATE ON THE ESSENTIAL

Desperately searching for a way to get his executives' work load under control, Bethlehem Steel's Charles Schwab once challenged consultant Ivy Lee: "Give us something to break the bottleneck and get the things done that need doing around here and you can name your own price."

"I can give you something that will take only a few minutes a day and pep up your 'doing' by half," Lee promised.

"Shoot!" said Schwab.

And this was Lee's advice: "In the order of their importance, jot down on a piece of paper the most urgent jobs currently facing you. Tomorrow, dig right in on priority job number one and stick to it until it is done. Tackle job number two in the same way; then number three and so on. Don't worry if you only finish one or two by the end of the day—you'll be concentrating on the most urgent ones. If all your chores can't be done by this method, the odds are overwhelming that they couldn't be by any other method. Make this a daily routine. When you're convinced that it works, pass it on to your executives. Have them use it for as long as you wish and ask for a report on results. Then send me a check for whatever you think it's worth."

Four weeks later Schwab sent Lee a letter of thanks for "the most valuable lesson" of his life, together with a check for $25,000.

What worked for Schwab, his executives and his company can work for you. Try it! It may revolutionize your life.

5. MOTIVATE YOURSELF

We do best the things we *want* to do. They almost always take precedence over the things we *have* to do. It follows that if you can somehow turn "have-to" chores into "want-to" ones, your performance will increase almost automatically.

Happily, you can achieve this through self-motivation. By creating the propelling impetus for achievement within yourself, you release all the potential in you. You enjoy your work.

You tackle it vigorously. And, most importantly, you get it done.

How can you create this self-propulsion? In two ways.

(a) REWARD YOURSELF. Put a "price" on the successful completion of every task and pay off without fail. Maybe a good cigar for a small task, supper out for a bigger one, a weekend trip for a blockbuster. The important thing is to set a "prize" that you know you want, then aim for it.

(b) PUT YOURSELF ON THE SPOT. Brag a little. Commit yourself by announcing what you are going to accomplish to people you'd hate to let down: your wife, boss, and friends. The very human desire to "save face" will do the rest.

6. ESTABLISH DEADLINES

Another effective way to commit yourself, if only to yourself, is to set specific time limits for specific achievements. It is one thing, for example, to say, "I'll finish that proposal as soon as I get a chance"; quite another to decide, "I'll finish that proposal before I leave the office tonight." In the first instance, you are setting the stage for procrastination and excuses; in the second instance, you are pinpointing a time by which you will accomplish a particular task.

In establishing deadlines for accomplishment, watch for two things:

(a) MAKE YOUR DEADLINES REALISTIC. If you don't, you will fail to meet them and, consequently, grow discouraged and give up.

(b) STICK TO THEM. Do *not* indulge yourself by rationalizing your failure to meet them, granting yourself extensions, coddling yourself. To the contrary, be as firm with yourself as you would be with a subordinate who promised to do something by a certain time or date. Once you have determined your deadline, move heaven and earth to meet it.

7. BE DECISIVE

Don't be so afraid of making a mistake that you do nothing. "Success," it has been said, "consists of being right 51 percent of the time." Once you have all the pertinent facts before you, therefore, reach a decision and *act*. And once you have acted, don't waste time in fruitless speculation over the wisdom of your decision. Go on to other things.

8. LEARN TO SAY NO

If you don't, you'll find yourself lured into doing things and going places you would really rather not. Part of your self-discipline and time-saving program should consist of separating the wheat from the chaff. Sure, go bowling or to a ball game, if you feel the need to relax occasionally. But avoid pointless commitments if you can spend the time more profitably elsewhere.

9. DON'T FALL INTO THE "TELEPHONE TRAP"

You can't beat the telephone as a time-saving way to get information, clear up misunderstandings, issue instructions and make appointments. But it is also an ever-present temptation to waste time through pointless gossip, social chit-chat, and the like. Protect yourself by knowing *in advance* what you want to accomplish with a call, with whom you wish to speak, the telephone and extension numbers involved, and then keep your call on a business-like level.

A personnel director explains this system thus: "In order to make all my telephone calls as brief and efficient as possible, I jot down all the points I want to discuss before I even pick up the phone. Below each point, I leave space to write in information I obtain during the call. When I hang up, I have a memo virtually ready to be typed and put in a file or turned over to an assistant for action. I find this method one of my best time-savers."

10. HANDLE THE MOST DEMANDING TASKS AT YOUR BEST HOURS

Each of us has a particular time of day when he is at his best. If you leap out of bed in the morning, your "prime time" is probably in the morning. If you don't feel like yourself before 11 A.M., you're probably an afternoon person.

Schedule your most difficult task for one period or the other. You'll slice many minutes off the time it otherwise might take to complete this work. You may even find it worthwhile to rearrange your entire work schedule, depending on your particular circumstances.

11. FOR THAT BIG JOB, MOVE UP A MEAL

Frequently, we run into periods when we have a job to do that requires everything we have. When that happens to you, try eating a heavier breakfast than usual, then skip lunch until 3 P.M. This gives you six uninterrupted hours to accomplish tasks. You eliminate the time usually wasted winding up your morning, waiting for a table or service during the busy lunch hour and the effort needed to get going after lunch. This midday period is also likely to have the fewest phone and other interruptions.

On the other hand, if you have a lot to do in the afternoon and into the evening, and too little time in which to do it, try eating a heavy late lunch and not dining until 8 or 9 P.M. You avoid the rush traffic home and get the quiet of an unoccupied office in which to operate.

Obviously, you can't follow this kind of schedule every day. But used with discretion, the straight-through schedule can often uncork bottlenecks, make a whole string of extra hours for you.

12. GET THE PENCIL-AND-PAPER HABIT

There are few more profitable investments a busy man can make than to buy a 25¢ notebook. Anyone who has ever experienced the "agony of recall" will vouch for the wisdom of jotting down reminders of things to be done: bright, but fleeting, ideas; appointments; telephone numbers. Strategically placed notes to yourself (on your bureau, mirror, car sun visor, desk) help keep you on top of all the "little" jobs you are otherwise apt to forget. A pencil and paper can even save you thinking time. Have to reach a decision? Write down the facts involved, alternatives open to you—and decide. Save reference time by maintaining an up-to-date list of company experts you can consult, oft-used addresses and telephone numbers. In short, don't burden your memory if you can help it.

13. DISCOURAGE INTERRUPTIONS

Well-meaning friends and colleagues who like to gab can throw your best-intentioned deadlines for a resounding loss. You can keep their friendship, as well as your schedule, by letting them know in a tactful way that you are pressed for time. Some men find that shifting their furniture around a bit works for them; others rearrange their lunch hour so that they are on the job while their colleagues are out eating. If your office is too inviting, try facing the wall or working with your back to others.

14. LISTEN

You'll avoid costly errors, backtracking and doing things over if you get instructions and information right the first time. Rush to a 3 o'clock meeting under the impression that it's scheduled for 2:30 and you're killing valuable time. Before you act, therefore, be sure you have all the facts—where, when, how, who, and why. If in doubt, ask.

15. LOOK FOR SHORTCUTS

A lot of men are the victims of status quo thinking. Just because they have always done a certain job in a certain way, they assume that it is the best possible method. Yet, almost any activity can be performed more efficiently with a little thought.

If you now do ABCD, try ACBD; it may be faster. Review your work pattern step-by-step and challenge each step with the simple question, "Why is this done?" Chances are you'll uncover needless details, some plain foolishness. How about delegating some of your more routine chores? Can you utilize any office machines (e.g., automatic typewriters, copiers, dictating equipment) to save time? How about finding out how others are saving time and adopting their shortcuts?

16. DO IT NOW

Before getting down to business, many of us will rearrange our desks, sharpen all the pencils in sight, gaze out the window, take a stab at the daily crossword puzzle, have a cup of coffee, sneak a look at the sports page, and then wonder where the time has gone. It may be human nature to procrastinate, but it sure is unproductive! Once you know what you have to do, *do it* as soon as you can. There is no trick involved here. Just dive in and do it. No one but you can help you lick the habit of putting things off. Do it. Do it *now*.

17. TUNE OUT "EMOTIONAL STATIC"

Most of us are aware of the obvious ways in which we waste time. What we tend to overlook are the emotional time-wasters in our lives, those feelings that burn up energy and make concentration on the job at hand much more difficult than it should be. Here are the main culprits, along with suggestions for effectively combating them:

(a) FRUSTRATION. If you want to burn up your energy three or four times faster than normal and dull your enthusiasm completely, be frustrated. But if you want relatively smooth sailing on the job, then treat frustration as a normal development in your life. Expect a quota of such problems and tackle them as you would any other problem. Analyze them, study them and, if necessary, sidestep them for the moment and turn your attention to something more promising until there is a better time to do the job.

(b) IRRITATION. Here is an energy sapper that can be destroyed simply by putting it into proper perspective. Analyze the cause. Is it worth the energy you're expending?

(c) IMPATIENCE. Fret about the time you're losing while waiting for a report, a telephone call, or even your wife and you burn up a lot of energy unprofitably. But put the same energy to work on some project or plan and, presto! you turn waiting time into productive time.

(d) WORRY. This is a common complaint in a tense world filled with threats, puzzling economic trends, tougher competition. Worry is largely the result of mentally turning "might happen" into "will happen"—a senseless thing since the chances are roughly fifty to one against the unpleasant eventuality occurring. Even if it does, why not consume the energy once instead of doubling that consumption by worrying in advance? This doesn't mean ignoring eventualities. But having taken all possible steps to guard against trouble, what's to be gained by worrying about it?

As a general antidote, try *action*. This doesn't only give mental relief; it stimulates your resourcefulness and opens up new and perhaps unexpected paths. As a final thought, so-called trouble frequently turns out to be a blessing in disguise. So why worry?

18. STREAMLINE HANDLING OF CORRESPONDENCE

Answering letters promptly, for example, not only gets them out of the way; but because many executives don't exercise this courtesy, you're also likely to make a good impression on correspondents.

One way to make this job as easy as possible is to jot down the gist of your reply on a memo pad while you read a letter. When you dictate the reply, you'll have an immediate reminder of what you wanted to say. For that matter, your secretary may be able to answer the letter on the basis of your notes.

The creation of form letters can also be helpful. Much of the correspondence you receive falls into several broad categories: queries, for instance, or requests for information. You can save yourself a great deal of time if you frame paragraphs or whole letters of response to use as needed. If the letters are well written, they'll sound more natural and courteous than a reply dictated in haste. An additional bonus: this procedure saves both you and your secretary time you would both normally devote to dictation.

A good secretary, of course, is a time-saving asset. Many of the letters you receive are doubtlessly job applications, social invitations, requests for charitable contributions and the like. By delegating the responsibility for replying to such letters to her, you immediately relieve yourself of a great deal of routine letter writing and free yourself for more creative work.

19. USE ALL AVAILABLE TIME

You can add substantially to your productivity by taking full advantage of all the time you have. This means *using* your travel time, waiting time, eating-alone time for such activities as planning your day, thinking out problems, catching up on your reading and getting ideas on paper for later implementation.

20. GET A JUMP ON TOMORROW

One of the biggest stumbling blocks to individual achievement: the all-too-human tendency to postpone a job. To avoid this wasteful procrastination, use reverse strategy—*start tomorrow's task today*. In the morning, you will get a psychological lift from finding the task already begun, be better prepared to plunge right in and finish it.

In reality, you will be taking advantage of a well-known psychological fact: our memory for uncompleted tasks, sparked by the unresolved tensions they create, is ten times greater than our memory for completed or unstarted ones. When you leave a job unfinished, your subconscious—that silent ally always on duty—goes to work on it. Later, when you return to the job, you are often amazed to discover that you have a whole new arsenal of ideas, insights, and solutions from which to draw.

21. POLICE USE OF LEISURE TIME

If going fishing with friends helps you relax—fine! Such activities can be true tonics. But don't do things just because others do them. We could all save hours a month if we were just a little choosier about the movies we attend, the TV shows we watch, the books and magazines we read.

22. VARY ACTIVITIES

Fatigue almost never attacks the entire body. Usually, it strikes only certain muscles at a time. By alternating your jobs, you can beat that tired feeling, get more done. Thus, if you have been sitting for several hours and are beginning to feel stale, switch to a stand-up job or one that requires walking. Been on your feet all day? Tackle a desk job. Not only will you find that your body can take more than you thought; the switch in jobs will keep you mentally alert, interested in what you are doing, and more efficient.

23. LEARN FROM MISTAKES

At the end of each day, some executives use pencil and paper to plan the next day's activities. But the vice president of a New York brokerage firm goes one step further: he writes down all the ways in which he's wasted time. He says this approach keeps him from repeatedly wasting time in the same ways and reports it's increased his efficiency by at least 50 percent.

24. CULTIVATE RESPECT FOR TIME

If you earn $20,000 a year for 50 forty-hour weeks, your time is worth ten dollars an hour. Get the habit of setting a mental price on your time and you will gain new respect for it. Such an approach will also help you judge whether it is really worth your while to tackle many of the minor jobs that may currently be eating into your workday. You wouldn't buy a couple of golf balls, then purposely throw them away. Why show any less respect for so irreplaceable a possession as time?

There they are: twenty-four ways to get more done in less time. Take each one to heart, practice what they preach, and you will find yourself in a new world—a world in which your days are marked by solid accomplishments and where time is no longer a feared enemy.

Chapter Three

Read Faster, Read Better

In case you haven't noticed, you are doing more reading in the line of duty than ever before. Books, magazines, journals, reports, technical papers, abstracts—all have dramatically increased in number. And the end is nowhere in sight.

As the sum total of human knowledge grows, more and more of it is being committed to the printed page. Just to keep abreast of the latest developments in your own field as this Age of Information swings into high gear and gathers momentum, you doubtlessly find yourself called upon to read more than you ever dreamed possible.

At the same time, the speed at which you read has, in all probability, remained fairly constant since your school days. If this is so, then clearly you are destined either to fall ever further behind as the gap between the amount to be read and your ability to read quickly and with comprehension widens, or to spend an increasingly greater part of your time in reading. Unfortunately, there is a built-in limit to the amount of reading time at your disposal.

There is only one solution. If you are to keep on top of the reading demands made of you, you must literally learn to "gobble up" the printed word and sharpen your ability to understand what you read.

What follows should help you reach this double goal.

HOW FAST DO YOU READ NOW?

Few people really know how fast they read. Yet, you cannot determine the extent of improvement needed in any area unless you know your current level of competence.

Here is a brief excerpt from a magazine article that is moderately difficult—roughly the kind you are apt to encounter in your regular business reading. Make sure you read it *exactly as you always read*, that is, at your usual rate and for comprehension.

It is important that you time yourself accurately, so use a watch or clock with a sweep second hand. You will find a simple chart at the end of the selection to help you determine your reading speed.

START

Right after World War II, while a graduate student at the business school of a "large eastern university," I was exposed to the writings of Elton Mayo. Mayo was a pioneer in applying the techniques, insights and words of the social sciences to business. Some time after Mayo discovered business, my classmates and I discovered Mayo. With his vast erudition and many years of experience in sociology and psychology—and in just plain living—Mayo used his words soundly, and well. But one could not say the same for me or for many of my *peer group*. We began to speak of *total situation*, of *established society*, and of *adaptive society*, of *group* and *rabble hypothesis*. Developments were generally *emergent*, and best of all we loved that wonderful word, *hubris* (a favorite of the New York *Times* book review for a couple of decades).

We used such words to impress teachers and classmates without really understanding what we were talking about. It was Ralph Hower, a great teacher, who brought us back to earth. He and some of his Harvard colleagues called them "buzz words"—they made a pleasant buzzing sound in our ears when we rolled them on our tongues but communicated very little to the hearer about the subject under discussion. We thought they were tremendously impressive, but Professor Hower pointed out that we were impressively saying nothing.

This experience brought me up short. Ever since, I've been a constant observer of my own use of buzz words and of their use by businessmen and business writers.

Buzz words, I've found, may overwhelm you into believing that you know what you're talking about when you don't; but your audience may suspect the truth. To a business writer, such a fate is not of great concern, since words are the end of his efforts. For the businessman, however, action is the end of his efforts; and if he has said nothing and does not realize it, he may fail to get action, or may get action he did not bargain for.

When a buzz word is so often used that it ceases to impress (*hubris* still gets them every time), it may become a useful part of the businessman's verbal baggage. This has been the good fortune of many of Elton Mayo's words. such as his special meanings for: *listening, emotional release, upward communication, social skills* and *social groupings.**

STOP

Time required: _____ min., _____ sec.

Time Chart

Time	Words per Minute
30 sec.	800
40 sec.	600
50 sec.	480
1 min.	400
1 min., 10 sec.	341
1 min., 20 sec.	300
1 min., 30 sec.	267
1 min., 40 sec.	240
1 min., 50 sec.	218
2 min.	200

* From Thomas H. Barton, "Eloquently Put, Sir . . . But How's That Again?" *Think* Magazine, March–April 1970 issue, p. 25. Reprinted by permission from *Think* Magazine, published by IBM, Copyright 1970 by International Business Machines Corporation.

You now know, perhaps for the first time, how fast you read. If you are dissatisfied with what you have discovered, here is how you can read faster and better, regardless of the nature of the material.

GET A BIRD'S–EYE VIEW

You wouldn't dream of starting out on a cross-country drive without first arming yourself with a map, an overall picture of the land to be traversed. Why? Because you want to avoid taking wrong roads or turning left when you should be turning right. In short, you want to arrive at your destination as quickly and safely as possible.

Similarly, when reading new material, it is extremely helpful to get a rapid bird's-eye view of the whole before settling down to mastering its specific parts.

There are three ways to do this:

1. DETERMINE ITS ORGANIZATION

Carefully examine a book, chapter or article before reading it thoroughly. Read introductory material and the summary or conclusion if there is one. If it is a book, study the table of contents which capsulizes the author's organization; read the introduction or preface in which the writer explains the nature and purpose of the book; and read the final, summarizing chapter. If you are dealing with just one chapter of a book or an article and it is divided into sections—possibly subsections— study the organization by glancing at the subtitles.

2. SKIM

This is the skill that gives an "aerial view" of the printed page. Drive yourself through a chapter in a book, an article in a magazine, a lengthy report, reading only the first sentence of each paragraph. Before long, you will be aware that this procedure makes sense, that the thought is flowing smoothly and with logic. If you find that the first sentence of each paragraph doesn't make sense or lacks continuity, try the last (some writers prefer "wrap-up" sentences to topic sentences). When you have finished, you will be aware of two things. First, you will have obtained an overall view of the entire selection. Second, you will have read *thoughts*, not just words.

Most people feel guilty if they don't read everything on a page. But effective skimming demands an aggressive new attitude: you must be willing to pass over a page without reading every word and without feeling guilty because of what you've skipped. Skimming, in short, requires a kind of visual recklessness.

You will have to learn to use a new pattern of eye movements, too, sweeping your eyes from the top to the bottom of the page, instead of horizontally. With some practice, you'll find that you can read vertically almost as easily as you can horizontally. The result will be that when your eye pauses on the page, instead of looking just to the left and right, you will also look up and down, thereby doubling the amount of reading matter you are visually able to consume at a single glance.

Strange as this technique may seem, it does work—with practice. Try it on the following excerpt from a newspaper story.* Force your eyes to follow the line down the middle of the story, relying on peripheral vision and some guesswork to fill in the details. At first, you will miss some—perhaps most— of the meaning. Gradually, however, as your eyes grow accustomed to following a north-to-south reading path, you will discover that your brain is catching on, too.

Force yourself to read your newspaper in this manner for the next several weeks. When you feel fairly comfortable with the technique, use it in your book and article skimming, too.

---

* From Eric Pace, "International Group Begins Study to Predict Air Pollution Levels," New York *Times*, May 18, 1970, page 5. Copyright © 1970 by The New York Times Company. Reprinted by permission.

PARIS, May 17—Will Paris's air sting a stroller's eyes in 1980? Will dust storms still sweep west Texas? Will smoke hang over the Ruhr?

By piecing together the answers to thousands of similar questions, a team of scientists based in Paris plan to frame an over-all prediction of just how serious and expensive the air pollution problem will become for much of the world in the decades to come.

The study began here last week at the gleaming new headquarters building of the Organization for Economic Cooperation and Development.

The 22-nation organization is running the two-year undertaking as part of its increased involvement in environmental affairs. The recent uproar about pollution in Europe as well as the United States has spurred various international organizations to put more money and manpower into environmental projects.

The North Atlantic Treaty Organizations has been looking into ocean pollution, among other problems, and the Council of Europe is holding a series of conferences on the environment.

Study to Use Computers

What the O.E.C.D. plans is to use computers and a small staff of experts to collate and standardize data about air pollution problems — and solutions—gathered by officials of the member countries. They range from Austria to the United States and from Ireland to Turkey.

The data will include information about the costs involved in using different devices to reduce pollution, and in using alternative fuels.

"Our aim is to help governments formulate their energy and air abatement policies," said Hilliard Roderick, an American physicist who heads the organization's division of

3. READ "TELEGRAPHICALLY"

If, after skimming, you decide that you want to read with more thoroughness, you can still save time by rereading the entire piece "telegraphically." That is, look for words within the paragraph that express ideas without adding unnecessary detail. For example, read the following:

> Recent studies appear to confirm what a lot of psychologists have long suspected: there is a definite and positive correlation between a person's grasp of the meanings of words and success. One expert explains it this way: "The answer seems to be that words are the instruments by means of which men and women grasp the thoughts of others and with which they do much of their own thinking. They are the tools of thought." In short, a good vocabulary represents *power*—power to communicate, understand and persuade. It is one of the weapons in your competition for personal advancement.

How many words did you read? There are 100 words in that selection and, unless you are a skillful reader, you probably read all 100 of them. Here, however, is what you should have read, "telegraphically":

> STUDIES CONFIRM PSYCHOLOGISTS: CORRELATION BETWEEN PERSON'S GRASP OF MEANINGS OF WORDS AND SUCCESS. EXPERT EXPLAINS: "WORDS ARE INSTRUMENTS BY WHICH MEN GRASP THOUGHTS OF OTHERS AND DO OWN THINKING." GOOD VOCABULARY REPRESENTS POWER—TO COMMUNICATE, UNDERSTAND, PERSUADE. ONE OF WEAPONS IN COMPETITION FOR PERSONAL ADVANCEMENT.

You have lost nothing of the thought, but you have reduced your reading load by more than 50 percent!

DECIDE WHAT YOU ARE LOOKING FOR

Let's continue our map analogy. If you are driving from New York to San Francisco and are interested in the most direct route, you will ignore those parts of your map that contain states through which you will not be passing. You probably won't even look at the New England or Southern states, for example, because they are of no importance so far as your New York–San Francisco trip is concerned. On the other hand, you *will* be interested in such states as Pennsylvania, Ohio, Indiana, and Illinois, for they lie directly between you and your destination.

The same holds true for reading matter.

Almost every book or article you read will contain a great deal of material a) you already know, b) you have neither desire nor need to know, c) you can easily grasp after one reading, and d) is explanatory and illustrative in nature so that you need not dwell upon it once you have digested the main idea.

The "bird's-eye view" that you achieve through determining organization, along with skimming or reading telegraphically tells you quickly what the material at hand covers.

Your question now becomes, "What, specifically, do I wish to get out of this welter of material?"

If, for example, you are studying the economy of Japan, you may pick up a book called *Introduction to Japan*. A "bird's-eye view" of the volume will tell you quickly that this book deals with many subjects besides economics: Japan's history, its social customs, its traditions, its religious beliefs, its politics, and so on. But right now you are only interested in its economy, so you quickly isolate those chapters and pages that are pertinent to your interest. Saved are many hours of irrelevant reading.

You must constantly keep in mind exactly *why* you are reading—what, precisely, it is that you wish to learn. And if you find your attention or interest wavering, you must consciously pull your mind back into focus. If it wavers ten times, pull it back eleven times. If it wavers twenty times, pull it back twenty-one times.

USE A PENCIL

Reading business material swiftly *only for the sake of speed* is senseless. Your primary aim should be to master what you read.

This is where the judicious use of a pencil as you read can be of incalculable aid. It makes a book or article irrevocably yours, for with it you impose your own thinking upon the contents. It gives you the feeling of having, to some extent, collaborated with the author. By compelling you to keep your eyes peeled for the important and the difficult, it keeps you mentally alert. And it takes the printed word off its pedestal and puts it in its proper perspective as a tool that is meant to be used.

There are several ways to mark reading matter. Some suggestions:

UNDERLINE

As you read, underline topic sentences or key words and phrases so that the gist of the material is immediately clear. Many accomplished readers underline important dates, names, technical terms and summaries of arguments or points of view. Once you get the underlining habit, however, you must guard against overdoing it; otherwise, you defeat its very purpose, which is to synopsize a paragraph, page, or section.

VERTICAL-LINE

Sometimes you will find a series of sentences or a paragraph of special relevance. In such a case, you can save time by drawing a vertical line in the margin next to it, with perhaps a double line for something of exceptional import. Later, you can study it at length.

JOT DOWN COMMENTS

Frequently, you will find sections with which you disagree; that remind you of what another writer said; that trigger a sudden insight of your own. Before you forget them, write a brief

note to yourself in the margin (e.g., "No evidence for this conclusion," "Anderson disproves this," "Try this in our own department?"). Occasionally, you will find that the most expres-
sive comment you can make is via punctuation. An exclamation mark can call attention to something important or astonish-
ing; a question mark, to something that you doubt or do not
understand. If they serve the purpose, use them.

TEST YOUR UNDERSTANDING

Most people are too kind to themselves. They give themselves
the benefit of every doubt. In learning, this most often takes
the form of rationalizing incomplete mastery of a subject with
some such balm as, "Oh, I get the general idea."

Frequently, though, the "general idea" is not enough—or is
wrong. You must train yourself to get to the heart of the matter
you are trying to learn. And, like most skills, this takes practice.

One excellent method of training yourself to spot important
ideas and separate them from the less important or merely
substantiating material is to write out a synopsis of what you
read, thus making it your own intellectual property. By getting
down the gist of the author's thesis or argument right away,
you enjoy the advantage of immediacy—at the moment of writing, the subject is clear in your mind. And since you cannot
paraphrase before you comprehend *what* you are paraphrasing,
by recasting his thoughts in your own words, you compel yourself to understand what the author has said.

Some book readers find it convenient to jot down their
synopses at the end of chapters, where there is usually some
space, or on the blank front and end pages of the volume. Others prefer to insert index cards or small slips of paper, which
they later staple inside the book or file away. Whatever procedure you choose or develop on your own, you will find that
once you form the habit, paraphrasing becomes a time-saving
guarantee of comprehension in the long run.

In order to reap the maximum benefit of this discipline,
keep your synopsis down to about one-tenth the length of the

original. Thus, your synopsis of a 2,000-word article should run approximately 200 words.

Try it. Take an article from today's newspaper and count the number of words it contains. Then read it through and write out your own "brief" of it.

Check yourself by rereading the original. Did you omit any important ideas? Did you insert any matter that is, strictly speaking, of secondary importance? Could somebody who had not seen the original get a fairly accurate idea of the author's point of view or the essence of the information he is reporting from your synopsis?

Sure, this takes time, but nothing you can name will so develop your "understanding muscle" as the continual testing of it. And, with repetition, you will find yourself getting only the "meat" out of everything you read.

In time, *all* these techniques will become second nature to you. But until they do, use them consciously. In the process, what used to be a chore will turn into a challenge. And you will be reading faster, remembering more.

Chapter Four

The Right Way
to Delegate Authority

You've seen him: the boss who is frantically working on Wednesday's chores when Friday rolls around. Panic-stricken, he cannot do his best; in despair, he makes bad decisions, takes out his frustrations on employees, and turns out—or overlooks—slipshod work.

You've seen the other kind, too: the boss who carries every bit as much responsibility as his disorganized colleague, but who has mastered the technique of passing out bits of it to others. He trusts them to make their own decisions within the framework he establishes for them. They report to him on results, not details, unless they need help with those details. You will find him busy, but not too busy to sit back and think.

Which one do you think gets more work done? Enjoys his job more? Is more respected by his fellows? Has the better chance of living to a ripe, old age?

There's really no contest, is there?

Why? Because the "delegate-what-you-can" man enlarges his area of action and multiplies his own efficiency by the number of people he allows to help him. By giving others the opportunity to prove themselves, he encourages initiative and personal growth among his subordinates. In firm control of the overall picture, he isn't weighed down by a hundred petty, worrisome details. He gets more done in less time, with a minimum of personal wear and tear.

A LITTLE QUIZ

Think you needn't bother delegating authority in your work or business? Here's a friendly challenge—ten questions that will tell you quickly whether you are in the saddle, or whether your work is riding you.

1. Is your work piling up too fast?
2. Do you spend several evenings each week "catching up" with work?
3. Are you usually pressed for letter-answering time?
4. Do you find yourself with too little time to see people on business matters?
5. Do you lack time to relax?
6. Are you frequently late in meeting deadlines?
7. Are you habitually swamped by details?
8. Do you feel stale?
9. Are you worried about your work load?
10. Have you been irritable lately?

If you answered even one question affirmatively, you can profit from learning to delegate.

Here are the ways and means that work.

DELEGATE THE RIGHT DUTIES

At the outset, ask yourself: "Which of my regular daily duties can I delegate right now?"

Your immediate answer will probably be, "None." Nobody can do your job as well as you. Granted. Nobody *can* do your job as well as you can, but one or more of your subordinates can almost surely do it well enough. The point is, you have more important fish to fry. Given time and practice, your delegate will become quite expert—providing you are careful in choosing the right person and in training him. We'll consider who is the right person later. Right now, let's stick to the problem of *what* to delegate.

The first, logical step is to draw up an exhaustive list of the duties you perform daily. If you are only average, you will be amazed by their sheer number. If, for example, you are in business for yourself, a small part of your list might look like this:

1. Open place of business.
2. Check reports of subordinates.
3. Look over mail.
4. Answer letters.
5. Visit various departments, talk to supervisors.
6. Interview job applicants.

The second step is to separate those details that *only* you can do from those that someone else might do. Here are two suggestions.

A. RECURRING DETAILS

One world-famous executive learned to delegate his everyday details the hard way, after collapsing from overwork. During his convalescence, he worked out a plan for delegating the repetitious drudgery of his daily duties. And the leisure he got from applying this plan resulted not only in his complete recovery, but in building up his great commercial enterprise.

What, precisely, did he do? He simply divided his work into two parts:

1. Important chores that demanded his personal attention.
2. Routine details that he could delegate to others.

And he found that he could save *over* 30 *percent of his time* by delegating.

Suppose you adopt a similar plan. Taking the list of your duties that you have drawn up, rearrange them under two headings: *Details That Only I Can Do* and *Details That Others Can Do.*

Rewrite your list monthly. If you are delegating as you should, your list will change and grow, month after month. Keep your old lists and compare them with the new. Move slowly but steadily toward divesting yourself of all unnecessary detail.

Take the six items our typical businessman drew up above, for example. His rearrangement might look something like this:

Details That Only I Can Do	*Details That Others Can Do*
Check reports of subordinates	Open place of business
Look over important mail	Mail can be sorted by secretary
Answer important letters	Some letters can be answered by
Visit various departments, talk	secretary
to supervisors	Interview job applicants

Saved: A lot of valuable time that can be used to attend to more important things.

B. LESSER DETAILS

The higher you progress in your business or profession, the harder you work. Consider the man whose small service company gradually expanded. With the growth of his business, his personal responsibilities kept mounting. In desperation, he consulted an industrial engineer who showed him *how to simplify* his job.

When his firm had been small, he was obliged to attend to all the details: the purchase of supplies, the typing of invoices and statements, the management of his shop. As his business grew larger, it just didn't occur to him that he could delegate some of those details to his helpers.

Even after he had consulted the industrial engineer, he

found it difficult to "let go." But little by little he lightened his load, relaxed, and began to enjoy better health and a greater income. Through delegation he had transformed an over-balanced job into a well-balanced organization.

This kind of organizing through delegating applies to you, too. *Delegate the lesser details of your job to those who have lesser jobs under you.* That's really why they are there.

Most of your subordinates—75 percent of them, according to recent surveys—are anxious to assume new duties.

DELEGATE TO THE RIGHT PEOPLE

One of the finest of executive skills is the art of selecting the right men for the right jobs.

Here is a simple formula that will help: *screen your men carefully, study them at work, test them with problems, and encourage their independent thinking.*

Sound simple? It is. But it takes time and some detective work. Here are some clues to look for before you decide to whom you will relinquish part of your authority.

DOES HE WANT MORE RESPONSIBILITY?

If 75 percent of your subordinates want new duties, 25 percent do not. You will all be better off if you identify them at the outset. With a particular individual in mind, ask yourself: Does he show initiative in his present job? Does he look for ways to boost efficiency and cut costs? Does he rise to challenges? Is he interested in how departments other than his own operate? Is he self-confident? Your answers will tell you whether or not the will to assume additional responsibilities is there.

DOES HE POSSESS AN ACTIVE MIND?

If he does, he has the capacity to grasp a problem and, through creative thinking, to solve it. When you talk with him, he is alert to your every word and asks questions indicating he is thinking beyond your immediate subject to related ways of solving the problem at hand and its possible ramifications.

DOES HE HAVE SELF-DISCIPLINE?

The man who can discipline himself can discipline others. Such a man seldom shrinks away from the hard job or dawdles over the easy one. Rather, he tackles both with equal zest.

IS HE WELL ORGANIZED?

That is, does he plan his work week in general and his work day in particular? Does he keep on top of his job? If he doesn't, he is certainly not ready for additional duties.

CAN HE LEAD OTHERS?

An important quality for those who are to hold responsibility and authority is *leadership*. Don't theorize over this characteristic. Instead, give the man under consideration a specific task, in which he will function with all your authority and responsibility. This task should be specific and brief; for example, the rearrangement of furniture in an office, the organization of an employee safety committee, a survey of employee morale. The more specific the task, the better your chance of sizing up his true potential.

DOES HE INSPIRE CONFIDENCE IN OTHERS?

Contributing to the quality of leadership is the quiet sense of being in command that comes from a thorough knowledge of his specialty; enthusiasm springing from sound health and emotional stability; the ability to organize, plan and make decisions; and a full desire to go out of his way to help meet the situation at hand.

IS HE ARTICULATE?

This confidence which he inspires is made complete by his easy expression and use of the English language. He speaks forcefully, with a pleasant voice and manner and with a range of vocabulary that enables him to convey his ideas clearly.

IS HE FLEXIBLE?

With changing needs taking place almost daily in every growing organization, it is essential that a man placed on his own have the necessary flexibility of thought and reaction to respond to new and shifting situations.

DOES HE COOPERATE WITH OTHERS?

Capping these qualities is the ability to work smoothly with everyone in order to get the results he is seeking on your behalf. For in the final analysis, your delegate, like yourself, must be able to get results by working with and through people. This is one of your best indicators that you have found the right man for the job you want done.

DELEGATE AS TRAINING

As you delegate more and more of your work, you will begin to spot those employees who appear to have what it takes to eventually assume permanent jobs of increased responsibility.

Although the delegation of work is usually viewed simply as a means of sharing the executive burden with subordinates, it can serve another, even more important, function: the training of such people for bigger and better things. When you have identified a man with unmistakable potential, delegate to him the following types of duties:

DUTIES TO STRENGTHEN HIS WEAKNESS

Give him plenty of exercise to overcome his weakness. (It's assumed that aside from this weakness he fully deserves your confidence.) Watch his progress from a distance, if possible, so that he will not be too nervous about your supervision.

A VARIETY OF DUTIES

Statistics have shown that variety in the details makes the whole job more palatable. Give him duties to test his versatility and add interest to his job, but be careful not to overspice. Too many and too diverse details will overburden him and may kill his interest altogether.

DUTIES TO MAKE HIM FEEL IMPORTANT

Let him realize that he has been spotted as a "comer."

DUTIES LEADING DIRECTLY TO ADVANCEMENT

Nothing will improve a worker's efficiency so much as the knowledge that he is moving steadily toward better things. Let your subordinate understand not only *what* he is to do, but also *why* he is doing it.

DUTIES ARRANGED ON RISING SCALE

Make each hurdle a little higher than the last. This will lead him to success after success, until he is ready for promotion.

Don't forget to show confidence in your delegate. Most of us tend to live up to what others expect of us. Show your subordinate that you do not doubt his capabilities and he will move heaven and earth not to let you down. In the process, he will discover new strengths that even he didn't know he possessed.

DELEGATE AT THE RIGHT TIME

The right time to delegate, of course, is whenever you can. But there are special occasions when you can delegate to best advantage. These are:

WHEN YOUR WORK LOAD IS TOO HEAVY

You can't possibly do your best if you continually add to your number of tasks. Spread them around, reserving for yourself only those jobs that demand your personal attention. No need, for instance, for you to answer all calls, make out bills, deal with repairmen and the like.

BEFORE YOU ARE ABSENT

Going on a business trip or vacation? Don't wait until the last minute to delegate work. Instead, make plans for this delegation well in advance of your departure. Brief your assistant as to what *must* be done, what should be done if there is time, what can wait. Discuss *all* items in detail and get his point of view. Encourage him to do the work in his own way. Above all, take time to train your delegate *before the zero hour.*

WHEN YOU ARE IN LINE FOR PROMOTION

Moving up? Make sure someone is ready to step into your shoes. Indeed, if no one is available, you may not *be* promoted at all. To insure the efficiency of your understudy, spend some time with him each day teaching him your job. Give him a number of practical tests to determine his capacity for the job. And allow him plenty of time to get ready to take over your job. The best training, remember, is *training by doing.*

That's the proper way to delegate authority:

1. Delegate the right duties.
2. Delegate to the right people.
3. Delegate as training.
4. Delegate at the right time.

The real secret of getting things done, you might say, is to let subordinates peel the potatoes and set the table. That way, you free yourself to plan the menu. Net result: a better "meal" for all concerned.

Chapter Five

The Art of
Making Decisions

"Should we hire Jones?"

"From whom should we buy our supplies?"

"Is this the time to invest in stocks?"

Decisions, decisions, decisions! Every day, we choose between alternative courses of action—sometimes wisely, sometimes "otherwisely."

Some businessmen pride themselves on their ability to make hair-trigger decisions, on never delaying or holding up others. But arbitrary decisions made for the sake of "getting things settled" are often wrong and costly.

At the other extreme is indecisiveness, the inability to pick a course of action and see it through. Not only does the chronic hemmer-and-hawer suffer from his own lack of solid accomplishment and consequent loss of self-confidence; the productivity and enthusiasm of the people under him nosedive, too.

But when almost any business decision you can name involves hundreds, often thousands of dollars, how can you be certain that your decision is the best possible one?

The truth is, you can't. There is no 100 percent guarantee on the wisdom of any decision in life. But you can do the next best thing. You can take certain steps to raise the odds in favor of your decision being right.

Before you attempt to reach any decision, however, make sure it's necessary by asking yourself these questions:

"DO I HAVE TO DECIDE?"

That is, is there really a problem? The best way to find out is to get it down on paper, preferably in a single, tight sentence that spells out what you will lose if it is not solved. Be honest with yourself and see if you *can* do anything about it. In most cases you can, but if you can't, don't waste time beating your head against a stone wall.

"WHEN MUST I DECIDE?"

Is time critical or can you wait without compounding the problem's mischief? If you can wait, time alone may decide things for you. Or you may be better equipped to handle it in the future.

"WHAT ELSE DO I NEED TO KNOW?"

Do you have all the pertinent facts? If not, what is missing? Have you considered all the consequences of the facts? *Where* can you find out more? *Who* may be able to assist or advise you? Will your decision affect others? If it will, it might be wise to consult them.

"CAN I IMPLEMENT MY DECISION?"

If you lack the resources, manpower, or authority to put a decision into action, there is little point in deciding.

"WHAT SHALL I DECIDE?"

This, of course, is your final step, the "main event" that is necessarily preceded by the above preliminaries. With your facts and their consequences clearly in mind, you are prepared to grapple with the actual decision-making process. Any one, or more, of the following techniques that have worked for others may work for you.

LIST OF PROS AND CONS

This basic method has been best described by one of the most practical men the United States has ever produced, Benjamin Franklin. In his own words:

"My way is to divide a sheet of paper by a line into two columns, writing over the one *Pro* and over the other *Con*. Then during three or four days' consideration, I put down under the different heads short hints of the different motives, that at different times occur to me, for or against the measure. When I have thus got them altogether in one view, I endeavor to estimate their respective weights; and where I find two, one on each side, that seem equal, I strike them both out. If I judge some two reasons con equal to some three reasons pro, I strike out five; and thus proceeding, I find where the balance lies; and if after a day or two of further consideration, nothing new that is of importance occurs on either side, I come to a decision accordingly."

Next time you find yourself perched on the horns of a dilemma, try Franklin's approach. You may be surprised how well it works.

TALLY OF GAINS AND LOSSES

This is really an elaboration of the list of pros and cons. Here, however, you try to put a numerical value on each point.

Sometimes, this numerical value can be translated into dollars. But all problems do not lend themselves to cost study; and even where good cost data are available, other intangible considerations may be decisive or may overshadow the cost portion of the problem.

In the tally technique, therefore, you set up gain and loss columns for each proposed course of action. Some gains and losses, of course, are more important than others. Hence, you look over the list and decide which gain and which loss are most important. These each get a value of ten. Then you assign every other gain or loss a number, plus or minus, depending on its worth in relation to ten.

For example, suppose you are wondering whether or not to hire Jack Jones as a salesman. Using the tally technique, you might set up gain and loss columns with the following values:

Hire Jones		*Don't Hire Jones*	
Six years of selling experience	+10	Has never sold our type of product	−10
Earned $16,000 last year in commissions	+8	Has held four jobs in last eight years	−9
Good appearance	+7	Over-talkative	−6
Self-confident	+7	A bit young for our customers	−4
Enthusiastic	+6	Does not own a car	−4
Gets along with people	+5	Unmarried	−2
Enjoys travel	+3		
Total	+46	Total	−35

In this particular case, your tally indicates that the decision to hire Jones has a factor of +11 in its favor. You conclude that you ought to hire him.

While a tally of gains and losses is by no means an infallible technique (your assignment of values is necessarily subjective), it is one effective way of reducing the guesswork in a decision.

YOUR OWN EXPERIENCE

In searching for solutions, we often ignore the obvious. Yet, what is right in front of our noses may be just what we are looking for.

As a mature man, you have a vast reservoir of personal experience to draw from. You have faced dilemmas before and, in one way or another, have solved them. Seldom is a decision-demanding situation completely new. It almost always contains one or more familiar elements.

Suppose, for example, that you want to raise some money in order to expand the physical facilities of your business. Your problem: how? You may never before have needed so much money for such a reason, but in all probability you *have* needed money before and, somehow, have raised it. How did you do it then? What other methods of raising cash did you contemplate using at that time? (One of the ideas discarded then may be just what you need now.) To whom did you go for advice? (He may be able to help you now.) By asking yourself such questions, you may literally stumble upon the key to your decision. At the very least, such self-interrogation can prime the wells of your thinking.

To get the maximum benefits from a review of your own experience, try these "trigger questions":

1. Have I ever had to make a similar decision?
2. How did I go about it?
3. Was the decision reached an effective one? Why?
4. If it was a poor decision, what can I do to avoid repeating that mistake this time?
5. Who, if anyone, helped me make the decision before?
6. Can I call upon him again?
7. In view of the results of my previous decision, can I reasonably anticipate reaching a wise decision now?
8. How, precisely, does the present situation differ from the past one?
9. In view of these differences, what modifications should I make in my thinking?
10. Has the passage of time altered in any way the results I may reasonably anticipate from following my own precedent (e.g., interest rates are higher, there is more competition, rents have risen, markets have changed, etc.)?

SOLICITATION OF OPINION

Frequently, two heads *are* better than one. And three may be still better. This is true providing that you use the right heads.

Before you take your survey of opinion, therefore, ask yourself some questions about the people from whom you intend to get advice:

1. ARE THEY QUALIFIED?

If you're undecided about introducing a new product, don't ask your accountant for suggestions. On the other hand, if you are considering incorporating your business, don't expect authoritative advice from your salesmen. Make sure the man you are asking for help knows something about the problem.

2. DO THEY HAVE ANY VESTED INTERESTS?

If your decision will affect another man's authority, importance or self-interest, he is unlikely to be able to give you objective advice.

3. HOW GOOD HAS THEIR PAST ADVICE BEEN?

Past performance is a fairly accurate clue to future performance. Do the people you intend to survey have a good decision "batting average"? If they don't, what makes you think they can tell you what to do now?

When you have thus screened your sources, take your poll and draw up a "score sheet" on which you get their answers to three main questions: (a) What are the specific benefits to be achieved by making this decision? (b) What are the risks or possible losses? (c) What will be the effect on the company and on the department for whose work the person contacted is responsible? Under each of these questions jot down the reaction of each person contacted.

If you have polled the proper people, you should end up with a wealth of helpful suggestions at your fingertips.

TRIAL RUN

Sometimes, before implementing a decision that carries with it broad ramifications (e.g., an important policy change, a shift in assigned work, additional expenses), it is wise, and practical, to set up a test situation first.

If, for example, you are wondering whether or not to promote Smith to a position carrying larger responsibilities, try assigning him *one* of the new responsibilities in his old job. Then keep tabs on his performance. If you are thinking of carrying a new line of products, before going all the way, test customer reaction with a few items. If you are contemplating a new advertising theme, measure its effectiveness with some test advertisements.

Whenever possible, try out your decision on a small scale.

YOUR SUBCONSCIOUS

In any discussion of decision making, the part that the subconscious mind plays should not be overlooked. Study the problem before you. Saturate yourself with the facts. Review the alternative courses of action open to you. Then talk it over with yourself; that is, give your subconscious all the pertinent information and a chance to simmer with all its other recorded experiences. Eventually, it will tell you which is the best possible decision.

It may take an hour, a day, or a week. But sooner or later, while you're shaving, watching a ball game, or raking leaves, it *will* come through.

CHECK YOUR OBJECTIVITY

While each of the above techniques can help you make more objective decisions, none of them is foolproof.

An ever-present danger in the decision-making process is the temptation to let our thinking be guided by our desires, inclinations and emotions rather than by the cold facts. We believe that we assemble reasons, evaluate them and arrive at a conclusion, but in reality the conclusion too often precedes the premises. When a problem confronts us, we jump to a conclusion, then go back and seek reasons to support that conclusion.

Such rationalization is thought of as the process of justifying a decision that has already been consciously arrived at. But it goes deeper than that. The decision may not have been consciously arrived at, but your inclinations will favor a particular line of reasoning, a particular set of facts which leads to the desired conclusion or decision. Such a decision may not be wrong, but it should be suspect.

There is no easy formula for eliminating your emotions from your reasoning. It is only in recognizing this very human tendency to wishful thinking, by scrutinizing every conclusion that seems too pleasing, by making a conscious effort to reason dispassionately that you can free your mind for thinking that is thoroughly logical.

So even if you sincerely believe that you have reached your decision with clinical detachment, check it for subjectivity with such questions as:

1. "Is my decision suspiciously close to what I personally would like to do?"
2. "Was I angry, elated, depressed or otherwise out of emotional equilibrium when I made my decision?"
3. "Did I tend to consider only those facts that reinforced my personal inclinations and biases?"
4. "Have I consciously or otherwise avoided taking into consideration any information that has a bearing on this decision?"
5. "Does my decision violate plain common sense?"

If you can honestly answer each question with an unequivocal no, you are ready for the final step.

IMPLEMENT YOUR DECISION

Once your decision has been made and tested for detachment, act on it. Act on it as though it were the only possible course of action open to you. Justice Oliver Wendell Holmes once said that if the weight of evidence was on one side in any choice of action fifty-one percent against forty-nine percent, a man must take that course as though it were 100 percent. No other rule is possible.

Make your decision. Act on it. Don't look behind. Don't harbor regrets. Don't nourish former hesitations. What's done is done.

If you use the techniques described here, the chances are good that it will be well done.

Chapter Six

Creating Good Ideas

There was a time when people thought that the ability to create ideas was like the ability to wiggle your ears. Either you were born with it or you weren't.

We know better now. Experiment after experiment indicates that everyone is capable of originating ideas. But the same experiments underscore the fact that most of us don't realize anything like our true potential as "idea men" because we apparently lose some of our more uninhibited creative powers in the process of growing up.

As we mature in other ways, something happens to the soaring imagination of childhood that once so easily turned a cumulus cloud into a fire-breathing dragon or a darkened wood into Camelot. Too often, the creative spirit that we can recall having once possessed is quashed by a host of external forces.

There is, first, the almost continuous pressure we are under from a variety of sources to conform to some accepted behavioral norm, whether it comes from adolescent peers, our neighbors or our co-workers. In the course of life, various institutions join the conspiracy: schools, the armed forces, the company. The price we pay for acceptability is enormous—nothing less than our individuality. And when we curb our behavior according to society's demands, we inevitably also curb the thing that makes us most unique: our patterns of thinking. As a consequence, our creativity diminishes.

Then there is the mischief unintentionally wrought by the very democracy that helps us in so many other ways. We pledge our allegiance to the political concept of majority rule and promptly confuse it with an ethical truism. Yet, the fact that "the majority rules" does *not* necessarily mean that "the majority is right." In truth, history is replete with examples of the majority being most definitely wrong. But once we allow the majority to wear a halo in our minds, our ability to think iconoclastically and reason originally becomes first inhibited, then paralyzed and, finally, nonexistent.

However, we are learning more about the creative process almost daily and, as a profitable by-product, we are mastering methods to enable us to create ideas, almost at will.

The important thing to realize is that the creation of good ideas *can*—indeed, *must*—be learned.

How do you go about it?

First, you must understand how the mind develops a new idea. Second, consciously establish the kind of climate in which idea creation thrives. Third, practice the personal discipline that helps the process operate.

The process itself is relatively simple. It is based on association—the tendency of the mind to put together old, familiar ideas into new, fresh combinations. There *is* nothing new under the sun, but we have only scratched the surface of all the possible ways these old things can be combined. By changing the size, the shape or the use of a common object, for example, hundreds of "new" products are created annually. Ever see a crumb sweeper used on a tablecloth? It's merely the hand sweeper women use on their rugs reduced in size and minus the handle.

Clarence Birdseye ate some fish that had been frozen and thawed during a trip to Canada, borrowed from nature, and founded the frozen food industry.

A doctor, remembering how he signaled to childhood friends through a hollow log, reduced the log in size, modified its shape—and invented the stethoscope.

Rudolf Diesel found the final clue for his engine in the way a certain cigar lighter worked.

The fountain pen owes its existence to the fact that people who used pens always kept ink at hand. Somebody merely asked, "Why not combine them?"

In each case, the inventor *borrowed* an existing idea and altered it by rearranging or combining certain elements. This combining of old ideas into new ones can be accomplished in two ways—by accident and by design.

Do your combining by accident and you are lucky. Do it by design and you are an idea man.

COAXING AN IDEA INTO EXISTENCE

The question is, how can you train yourself to do it consciously and deliberately? What are the precise steps you ought to take in order to reweave your knowledge, experience and observations into fresh ideas and solutions? Here are some suggestions:

1. SHAKE OFF THOSE MENTAL SHACKLES

Creativity is frequently difficult because we unwittingly become the prisoners of our own thinking. Four roadblocks in particular commonly stand between us and a new idea. Get rid of them and you will liberate your ability to innovate. They are:

STATUS QUO THINKING. The vast majority of people tends to think, "This is the way things are because they must work best this way. If improvements could be made, they would already have been made by people smarter than I." It's a false assumption, of course. Almost anything you can think of can be improved in some way.

INERTIA. Most of us take the course of least resistance because it's the comfortable, lazy way. Yet, action breeds action. Take the first, deliberate step toward creative thinking—dissatisfaction with "things-as-they-are"—and it becomes progressively easier to think about better ways, do something about our thoughts, test the results, refine our ideas.

LACK OF SELF-CONFIDENCE. "Who am I to upset the apple cart?" This is the basic assumption that paralyzes fresh thinking. Who *are* you? You're one in four billion, that's who! There never has been—never will be—anyone quite like you! *That's* why you doubtlessly can bring a new approach to any problem.

FEAR OF RIDICULE. Closely allied to lack of self-confidence, the fear of having our ideas laughed at is another basic cause of timidity in creative thinking. Yet, consider four of our most unorthodox (and creative) minds—Galileo, Newton, Edison, Freud, all of whom were laughed at, even despised, at one time. But they stuck to their guns and lived to see themselves honored by those who scoffed. The laughers are usually a bit envious. so don't let them throw you.

2. IDENTIFY YOUR TARGET

What kind of an idea do you need? Exactly what is the problem? Unless you answer this concretely, you have no definite goal, without which your "creative juices" remain dormant. If you have only a vague feeling of discontent, a suspicion that something is wrong, but can't zero in on anything specific, try this proven technique—in terms of your own job, answer these questions:

What made me mad today?
What took too long?
What was the cause of a complaint?
What was misunderstood?
What cost too much?
What did we waste?
What was too complicated?
What was just plain silly?
What job required too many people?

What job involved too many motions?
What job didn't get done?

The answers will almost certainly give you a long list of needs. Once you have them, there you are with your specific targets.

3. BE A CREATIVE "COPYCAT"

Now is the time to do your borrowing and combining. Take stock of the ideas that interest you and see whether you can adapt any of them to your own needs by asking yourself questions like:

Can I make it larger?
Can I make it smaller?
Can I make it longer?
Can I make it shorter?
What if I did it faster?
What if I did it slower?
Suppose I add to it?
Suppose I subtract from it?
Shall I use more?
Shall I use less?
Should I change just one part?
Suppose I did it half as often?
Suppose I did it twice as often?
Should I make it higher?
Should I make it wider?

Should I make it lighter?
Should I make it heavier?
Shall I do it sooner?
Shall I do it later?
Could I use more parts or steps?
Could I use fewer parts or steps?
Might I use half as many?
Might I use twice as many?
Suppose I used a different shape?
Suppose I used a different color?
Suppose I did it backwards?

Your answers may amaze you.

4. THINK ABOUT IT INTENSELY

If your conscious efforts to combine old elements into a new idea are unsuccessful, don't grow discouraged. Tell yourself that you won't put your target out of your mind until you hit it. Then stick to your resolution until you either get the idea you're seeking or reach the limits of your "frustration tolerance."

5. FORGET IT

If you have conscientiously taken steps one through four, your subconscious will take over at this point.

6. BE PREPARED FOR A SUDDEN INSIGHT

Your subconscious may percolate for an hour or a month, making comparisons among known facts, marking some for possible use, setting others aside for future reference, rejecting others outright. With computer-like speed, it will dredge up old ideas and forgotten daydreams, looking for congruencies and relationships in the welter of raw material you've stored away over the years, investigating modifications, measuring possibilities, and weighing alternatives. Then, suddenly, unexpectedly, it will send to the surface an idea, or two, or five, or ten.

Because these insights are apt to come at the most unpredictable times in the most unlikely places and are, at best, fleeting in duration, be prepared to capture them on paper by keeping little stacks of cards or note pads in such key areas as your night table, telephone stand, automobile glove compartment, workbench, shaving mirror, coat pocket.

SOME WORDS OF CAUTION

In applying these techniques, bear the following in mind:

1. Be sure you aren't tackling too big a problem. A king-size dilemma can almost always be cut down to a series of smaller, more manageable ones.
2. Take on only one problem at a time. Try to juggle several simultaneously and you will grow discouraged, inefficient.

3. It isn't always necessary to solve problems in a logical, one-two-three step sequence. Skip over parts that won't yield and go on to some other section. Often this suggests the ideas you need for the part of the problem you temporarily bypassed.

4. Never be satisfied with a single idea, one solution to a problem. About the time the first idea comes along, your mind is just warming up, as a rule, and it is likely that a number of other ideas are forthcoming—if you encourage them.

5. Talk over your problems and your ideas with others. Their views may give you a fresh slant on things.

6. Keep trying. Samuel Johnson said it. You remember it. "There isn't a problem the human mind can devise that the human mind cannot also solve."

So much for the mechanics of idea creation. But in order for them to work, they require the proper climate. And it is up to you to provide it.

THE CREATIVE CLIMATE

Basically, three essential ingredients comprise the ideal climate for idea creation: *the incentive to produce ideas, the pressure to produce ideas* and *the willingness to accept ideas.*

First and foremost, therefore, see to it that you provide yourself with a compelling reason for creating ideas. Approach your task with a selfish, "What's-in-it-for-me?" attitude. Actually enumerate the rewards you will reap from the idea you are seeking. If necessary, write them out so that you can see them, black on white. Will you make more money? Get promoted? Beat the competition? Earn the praise of your superiors, colleagues, customers? In short, *make yourself thirsty for success.* Human nature will do the rest.

As important as incentive in producing ideas is pressure, a sense of urgency about getting the job done. Within reason, the pressure of deadlines, the demand upon ourselves for ideas within a certain time limit, helps to produce ideas and brings out our highest creative abilities.

Unless this sense of urgency is present, ideas will not develop in worthwhile quantity. We all tend to procrastinate and the development of ideas being the tough work it is, the tendency to dawdle here is a particularly strong temptation. The odds are that if you need one idea and have a week to produce it, you will produce it within the week. But if you need two ideas and have only one hour to produce them, your chances of getting the two ideas may be even better than getting the one. So give yourself a deadline and *stick to it.*

But providing yourself with the incentive to create ideas and bolstering your resolve by setting a deadline are still not enough. Strange as it may sound, you must also be willing to accept your new ideas.

It is seldom difficult to find good reasons why something new can't work. But almost every major innovation you can name came into existence because some determined idea man stubbornly stuck to his guns; for example, Morse, Fulton, Bell, Ford, and Salk. People who make their way with their minds almost always experience disappointments and go through times when it seems the better part of wisdom to give up. What separates the men from the boys is a bull-headed unwillingness to quit until they are proven conclusively wrong. They simply refuse to be discouraged by theoretical arguments against their ideas. This "show-me" attitude is just another way of describing the third requisite of the creative climate—the willingness to accept new ideas by the idea man himself.

This may sound like an indictment of judgment, but it isn't. Judgment evaluates ideas *after* we have them. But we cannot use judgment and imagination at the same time. To do so would be like applying the brakes to your car while hitting the accelerator. In both cases, the net result is that you go nowhere and waste energy in the bargain.

The secret is to operate these two parts of your mind independently. When you are after ideas, keep judgment out. Let your imagination run wild. Then—and only then—step in with judgment and decide on the value of the ideas your imagination has produced.

HOW TO JUDGE AN IDEA

At this point you are ready to render a verdict on the value of your idea. There are at least four questions about your brainstorm that you should be prepared to answer.

1. DOES YOUR IDEA YIELD THE DESIRED RESULTS?

In short, will it work? If it is designed to save time in a particular sequence of activities, for example, does it actually save time? Enough to make it a meaningful contribution? Since most ideas flunk this first test, be brutally honest with yourself. If the answer is no, don't give up. Keep working to improve the idea.

2. IS YOUR IDEA A GENUINE IMPROVEMENT OVER THE STATUS QUO?

Some ideas are impractical not because they don't work, but because even though they do, little is to be gained from implementing them. For instance, suppose you invented an aerosol container that was activated by a trigger instead of a button. Even if it worked as well as, but no better than, conventional aerosol containers, what incentive would an aerosol container manufacturer have to switch to your trigger? None. So make sure that your idea is better in some way than the idea it is designed to replace.

Some specific recommendations come from the U.S. Navy which, like any big organization, is on a constant alert for new ideas. To separate the wheat from the chaff for further consideration, it employs this ten-point check list which can be used by anyone who wants to know whether his latest brainstorm has possibilities. Try it on your very next bright idea.

(a) Will it increase production or improve quality?
(b) Is it a more efficient utilization of manpower?
(c) Does it improve methods of operation, maintenance or construction?
(d) Is it an improvement over present tools and machinery?
(e) Does it improve safety?
(f) Does it cut down on waste?
(g) Does it eliminate unnecessary work?
(h) Does it reduce costs?
(i) Does it improve present office methods?
(j) Will it improve working conditions?

If your idea rates at least one yes, then you probably have a constructive idea, according to the U.S. Navy.

3. IS IT TOO COSTLY?

Anybody can become a millionaire virtually overnight by coming up with an inexpensive process for extracting gold from the oceans of the world. That is no secret, for it is common knowledge that our seas contain millions of tons of gold. Unfortunately, no one has yet been able to devise a method of extraction that is less expensive than the value of the gold reclaimed. Since the world price of gold is currently $35.00 an ounce, even if you had a method that cost only $35.01 for every ounce extracted, your idea would have no intrinsic value because you would lose a penny on every ounce "mined." And what is true of taking gold from the sea is true of any idea. If its cost outweighs its benefits, it is not a good idea—yet. (This does not mean that it cannot be improved through additional work and thought.)

4. IS ITS TIMING RIGHT?

Because timing is often an important factor in the efficacy of an idea, examine your idea carefully from this point of view.

There would, for example, be little to be gained from an improved buggy whip in this age of 350-horsepower automobiles. In judging your idea, therefore, consider its timing. Are all the conditions affecting its practicality present *right now?* Is the idea too late? Too early? Does it rest on *assumptions* about the future? In short, remember that every idea must be operable in terms of the time within which it is to be implemented.

If your idea passes these four tests, you may safely judge it practical.

SAVE YOUR IDEAS

Even when you find that you cannot use an idea, don't throw it away. You've worked hard to produce it and, while it may not meet current needs, it may be just what you will be looking for tomorrow, next month, or next year.

So save it. Create an "idea bank," a central repository for *all* the ideas that you dream up. With a little tinkering, some further thought, the addition of some elusive "secret ingredient," any one of the ideas you deposit may be the million-dollar insight you will need some time in the future. You might jot your ideas down on 3 x 5 cards or build up a scrapbook of them. The important thing is to arrange them so that you can locate any particular item at a moment's notice.

And to keep your creative power growing, do what you would do to keep a savings account growing: *keep depositing.*

Come to think of it, there is frequently a very real relationship between the two.

For all the importance rightfully attached to imagination as a means of creating ideas and finding fresh solutions to problems, it is by no means the only tool at your disposal. There is another mental process, equally valid and frequently more demanding, that no discussion of the disciplines underlying effective self-management can ignore. It's called logic.

Chapter Seven

All about Logic

As a problem-solving, decision-making, communications-simplifying tool, logic is an indispensable part of an executive's basic equipment.

Yet, how much do you really know about it? What, precisely, *is* logic? How does it work? How can you use it to best advantage?

Like the hero of Molière's play *The Would-Be Gentleman* who was dumbfounded to learn that he had been speaking prose all his life, you may be surprised to discover that you use logic every day. You place your favorite humidor out of reach whenever the Coopers visit you with their children. Why? Because, through sad experience, you've learned that the Cooper children are destructive little so-and-so's. You avoid talking politics with Morgan. Why? Because in the past he has flown into a rage whenever his political views have been challenged.

You don't *consciously* employ logic in such situations, but if you analyzed the thought processes at work on these occasions, you would find that they go something like this:

> *Whenever the Cooper children visit us, they break something.*
> *The Cooper children are visiting us today.*
> *Therefore, they are going to break something today.*

In the case of the irascible Mr. Morgan, your thoughts probably run something like this:

> *Morgan got into a huff when Adams challenged his political views last week.*
> *Morgan fumed when Baker challenged his political views last month.*
> *Morgan exploded when Carter challenged his political views at the club.*
> *Morgan almost had a stroke when Drexler challenged his political views at this year's trade convention.*
> *Therefore, Morgan flies into a rage whenever his political views are challenged.*

There, in a nutshell, you have the two ways in which the human brain interprets facts and draws conclusions from them —*deduction* and *induction*. Together, they comprise *logic,* "the science of correct reasoning."

Since you want to think clearly about your problems and decisions, it is essential that you understand what these two forms of correct reasoning are, how they work and of what use they can be to you.

"ELEMENTARY, MY DEAR WATSON": WHAT DEDUCTION IS

One of the most memorable meetings of all time is surely that of Dr. Watson and Sherlock Holmes. Knowing absolutely nothing about the doctor, Holmes says, "You have been in Afghanistan, I perceive." Later, he explains how he arrived at that startling, but true, conclusion:

"The train of reasoning ran, 'Here is a gentleman of a medical type, but with the air of a military man. Clearly an army doctor, then. He has just come from the tropics, for his face is dark, and that is not the natural tint of his skin, for his wrists are fair. He has undergone hardship and sickness, as his haggard face says clearly. His left arm has been injured. He holds it in a stiff and unnatural manner. Where in the tropics could an English doctor have seen such hardship and got his arm wounded? Clearly in Afghanistan.'"

Naturally, Arthur Conan Doyle's immortal detective deduced all this in a split second. But, to take one detail only, this is the course his thinking must have taken:

> *Living in the tropics darkens a man's skin.*
> *This man's skin has been darkened.*
> *Therefore, he must have lived in the tropics.*

Holmes' chief weapon is deduction, that is, reasoning from a general principle to a particular instance. His thinking is based on the assumption that whatever is true of all instances or members of a class *must* be true of one instance or member.

Much of your thinking is like that, too.

HOW DEDUCTION WORKS

If, for instance, you know that all men drink water and that David Armstrong is a man, you deduce that David Armstrong drinks water. In the language of logic, the pattern of such a line of reasoning is termed a *syllogism,* consisting of a general statement called a *major premise,* a particular statement called a *minor premise* and an inference drawn from the two called a *conclusion.* Expressed as a syllogism, the above would look like this:

> *All men drink water* (major premise)
> *David Armstrong is a man* (minor premise)
> *Therefore, David Armstrong drinks water* (conclusion)

Obviously, nobody expresses himself in syllogisms. Nevertheless, our thought processes frequently follow the syllogistic pattern. You say, for example, "There ought to be a law against selling cigarettes to children because they can be harmed by them." In reality, you have thought your way through this syllogism:

*There ought to be a law against selling to children all
things likely to harm them.
Cigarettes are likely to harm children.
Therefore, there should be a law against selling cigarettes
to children.*

IF IT'S LOGICAL, IS IT TRUE?

A *logical* deduction is not necessarily a *true* one. If either of
your premises is untrue, your conclusion will be untrue, *although it may be perfectly logical.*

Deduction is merely a *method* of arriving at a conclusion.
That conclusion can be no truer than the premises on which
it is based. An example will clarify the matter.

*All men named Smith are of English ancestry.
John's last name is Smith.
Therefore, John is of English ancestry.*

Based on the major and minor premises, no other conclusion is possible. But the major premise is patently false. All men
named Smith are *not* of English ancestry. So the conclusion,
while inescapably *logical*, is untrue.

Similarly, it is crucial that your minor premise be true.
Consider this syllogism:

*All people who live on Grand Avenue are rich.
George Fowler lives on Grand Avenue.
Therefore, George Fowler is rich.*

If George Fowler has only pretended to live on Grand
Avenue, your conclusion does not follow. Only if he *truly* lives
on Grand Avenue and all people who live on Grand Avenue
are *truly* rich, must he be rich, too.

The essential point to remember—indeed, to engrave on
your mind—is that in order to be a really sure-fire problem
solver, the deductive process must start with a major premise, a

general statement, that is true *without exception*. And your minor premise, your particular statement, must also be true.

THE PROPER USE OF DEDUCTION

Let's assume that you want to invest some money, but aren't sure what to put it in. A friend tells you that people are making fortunes investing in computer stocks, so you decide to invest in them, too. Your deduction is based on this syllogism:

> *People who invest in computer stock make fortunes.*
> *I am going to invest in computer stocks.*
> *Therefore, I am going to make a fortune.*

Alas! You have overlooked the fact that your major premise is not true *without exception*. Perhaps a lot of people do make fortunes in computer stocks, but a lot don't. *All* people who so invest their money do not make fortunes.

Suppose you are facing the problem of diminished profits due to the higher prices you are paying for raw materials. Let us say that, in the course of gathering your facts, you learn from your purchasing agent that you can reduce the per-unit cost of your raw materials by buying them in larger quantities. You decide to increase the size of your future orders because you deduce:

> *Whenever one increases the size of an order for raw materials from any of his suppliers, his per-unit cost goes down.*
> *I am going to increase the size of my orders for raw materials from my suppliers.*
> *Therefore, my per-unit price will go down.*

And you're right! Why? Because not only are both your major and minor premises true, but your conclusion necessarily follows from them.

IN A NUTSHELL

Whenever you try to reach a 100 percent logically valid conclusion based on a fact or set of facts—

1. Be sure your major premise is true without exception.
2. Be sure your minor premise is true. Since this is always a particular statement, it should be relatively easy to check on its truth.
3. Be sure your conclusion necessarily follows from your major and minor premises.

"But," you may rightfully ask at this point "if the deductive process is supposed to start with a major premise, a general statement, that is true without exception, how can we be sure that *any* statement is absolutely true?"

Good question.

There is only one way: by observing many individual instances and eventually expressing a generality that covers every observed instance. Which brings us to

INDUCTION

For example, you throw a book up into the air; it comes down. You throw a feather up into the air; it flutters down. You toss a balloon into the air; it floats down. Everything you throw up eventually comes down. So you draw a general conclusion from your observation: "Whatever is thrown up, comes down." You adjust your actions to this general conclusion and, lo and behold, it works.

In reality, however, few inductions are perfect, for in order to be so, every instance to which the generalization applies would have to be observed. This is almost always impossible. You could spend your life throwing things up in the air and watching them come down, yet never be completely sure that this *always* happens. It is possible—though not probable—that at this very moment an Indian fakir is throwing a rope into the air and it is actually continuing to rise. Highly unlikely, to be sure, but just barely possible.

Only when you have observed every specific instance can your generalization be termed completely true. Take the major premise you employed in deducing that your per-unit price will go down if you place larger orders with your suppliers. You used that premise because your purchasing agent told you about it. How did he learn that it was true? If he checked every one of your suppliers and found that each offered reduced rates on larger quantities, his generalization was perfect. He observed *every* instance, then drew a completely true generalization.

Does this mean that induction can only be an aid to clear thinking when you have observed every single instance of a phenomenon? Not at all.

THE WORKING HYPOTHESIS

Even though you can rarely observe every instance of anything, you can almost always observe some instances and, from them, draw a *hypothesis,* a tentative generalization.

For example, you notice that, when you are trying to persuade employee A to use his safety equipment, he becomes genuinely interested in what you are saying when you show him a photograph of an injured worker who had neglected to use his safety equipment. So do employees B, C and D.

You hypothesize that other employees will be similarly impressed by the photograph and decide to play it up in future presentations. You do and they *are* impressed. Your hypothesis —your tentative generalization—works. If you later discover that the photograph does not impress *every* employee, you modify your hypothesis accordingly: "*Most* employees are impressed by the photograph." The probability of success still appears to depend to a great extent on showing employees the photograph.

AVOID THESE TWO TRAPS

Depending on what you are trying to generalize about, you will require one, a few, or many observations. If you are wondering whether you have the ability to jog a mile, one successful attempt will tell you. If you wish to generalize about the relationship between doing sit-ups and the acceleration of the human pulse, ten or twenty observations may be enough. If you are trying to determine whether a certain drug cures the common cold, however, even twenty successes would not be enough to generalize from, although they might make you hopeful. Three hundred might provide reason for optimism. Three thousand successes might be enough to generalize from, providing there are no failures, for even one failure negates the *without exception* that you are trying to establish.

The number of specific observations from which you can "build" a general statement, then, may vary from one to millions.

But let's be realistic. Only a scientist has the time, the patience or the resources to run thousands of experiments. The rest of us must be content with establishing a high probability of truth for our inductions.

Depending on what's at stake, too, we require different degrees of probability. It is less crucial to determine how accurate a rifle is if you are buying it for target practice than if you are responsible for purchasing weapons for an army. In the first case, ten practice shots might suffice to tell you that it is accurate enough for your needs. In the second case, where the protection of your country and the lives of thousands of men might conceivably be at stake, thousands of practice rounds might be required to establish the weapon's accuracy.

This brings us to the first trap awaiting the careless user of induction:

THE HASTY GENERALIZATION

Arriving at a generalization before observing a sufficient number of specific instances is one of the most common errors in reasoning. Your secretary makes a typing error on Monday. She mishandles a phone call on Tuesday. "That girl is stupid," you say. You've generalized on much too little evidence. Since hasty generalizations form unsound major premises, you can avoid trouble by asking yourself, "Have I considered a sufficient number of instances to warrant this conclusion?"

The second trap to avoid is:

THE UNREPRESENTATIVE INSTANCE

If you were trying to generalize about what happens to things that are thrown up in the air and you accompanied an astronaut on a trip to the moon, you would observe in his capsule that things thrown up in the air either stay where they are or float around. Because gravity is not at work in this special case, the reliability of your generalization would suffer. Unless the instances you examine are typical of the whole class under consideration, your generalization is thrown off course. The question to ask yourself here is, "Have I observed representative instances under representative conditions?" If your answer is no, you are building your generalization on sand.

USING THE TWO FORMS OF LOGIC

In order to solve most problems, you will have to use both induction and deduction. That's because some of the facts you dig up about your problem will be specific instances from which you will have to generalize and others will be more general instances from which you will have to "particularize."

You are, for instance, thinking of entering a franchise business but aren't sure of the field you will choose. Inherent in your thinking is the generalization that a franchise business offers opportunity. Research shows that Jones in Eastfield, Smith in Centerville, Peters in Westland and several others are doing very well with doughnut shops. By induction, you generalize, "Everyone who enters the doughnut shop franchise business earns a comfortable living." (You might be right or wrong, depending on whether you studied enough representative cases, but that is your generalization.)

In turn, this becomes the major premise for a logical deduction: "I am going to enter the doughnut shop franchise business. Therefore, I will earn a comfortable living." This is logically valid, remember, but not necessarily *true*.

Depending on the exhaustiveness of your research, the *probability of truth* of your conclusion will vary. Most thinking, most problem solving depends on probability. The proper use of logic is to "load the dice" in your favor as much as possible. Even though there is no guarantee that you will always be right, your chances of being so with logic are vastly higher than those of a man who rushes into a conclusion based on "hunch" or "feeling."

But don't expect to solve all your problems with logic alone. There is more, a lot more, involved in the problem-solving process, to which we now turn our attention.

Chapter Eight

How to Tackle a Problem and Solve It!

Engineer, manager, salesman, chief—regardless of your title, you are essentially in the problem-solving business.

Are you an executive? Then you must keep costs down, profits up, motivate those under you, make decisions almost daily.

A salesman? Then you must locate new prospects, convert them into customers, be prepared to answer objections, meet—and beat—the competition.

Is your work technical in nature? Then your job is one long search for better methods, materials, and processes.

In short, no matter how you earn your living, *your primary job is to tackle problems and to solve them.*

Nobody need tell you what tough work that can be. But it can be made a lot easier by adapting to your own needs the techniques developed and used by our most highly skilled and successful problem solvers: our scientists.

Their methods are no secret. For years, they have used them to unravel some of the world's knottiest problems, from the origin of disease to the conversion of matter into energy. And while they have experienced their share of failures, their problem-solving batting average has been, and is, incredibly high.

THE SCIENTIFIC METHOD

How do they do it? In a word, through *organization*. Over the years, through costly trial and error, scientists have discovered that problems are most readily solved through a particular sequence of actions. Follow this sequence yourself and, in eight cases out of ten, you'll come up with a workable solution to your problem. There are just seven steps.

1. ASSEMBLE THE FACTS

Visualize your problem as a large, heavy ball, too big to handle, and almost impossible to budge. Now picture that same ball with knobs all over its surface which permit it to be turned and examined.

Facts are *knobs* that permit you to "turn a problem around." They contribute to your understanding and, if properly assembled, these facts explain *why* the problem exists and *how* to solve it.

How do you go about assembling facts? There are three basic techniques:

(a) ASK QUESTIONS. Providing only that you ask the right people, there is no better way of getting the facts in any case. Make sure that the person you are asking has no reason *not* to tell you the complete truth (e.g., fear of your displeasure, hesitation to admit ignorance, lack of information, a vested interest of some kind). Quiz yourself, too. Sometimes we know the answers, but need questions to unleash our knowledge.

(b) KEEP EYES AND EARS OPEN. There is no substitute for first-hand observation. What you see with your own eyes and hear with your own ears is usually dependable. But beware of confusing opinion, prejudice, or rumor with fact.

(c) READ. Reading vastly expands your access to other minds, novel insights, diverse points of view, and experiences.

Over the years, we have all learned which printed sources of information are dependable, and which are not. It is a safety measure to check one authority against another, so read books, magazines, and newspapers. Since you will want the latest information, check the dates on your printed sources.

2. WEIGH THE FACTS

Some of the so-called facts that you uncover will prove less than true; others will shed no particular light on your problem. That's why you must subject every "fact" to a two-part test.

The first test is for *accuracy*. Have you been able to check each fact by personal observation? Expert testimony? Experimentation? Are any of your facts mutually exclusive; that is, does one flatly contradict the other? Questions like these will help you establish the validity of any fact.

The second test is for *relevance*. It may be a fact that your senior supervisor collects stamps, but it is doubtful whether that has any bearing on the poor performance he's turned in during the past two months. Perhaps the easiest way to assess a fact for relevance is simply to ask yourself, "So what?" If your answer is, "So—nothing," the fact in question is probably irrelevant. You can safely dismiss it from consideration.

3. PLAY WITH THE FACTS

In tackling a problem, the orderly assemblage and testing of facts are frequently not enough. They must be juggled, toyed with, turned upside down, hitched to nonfacts and handled whimsically, for the answers to problems can come from the most unlikely sources such as experience, experiment, accidents, daydreams, and hard work. You never can tell where or when you'll find them, but there are ways to coax them into existence. Some possible approaches:

USE YOUR IMAGINATION. Fresh ideas and novel solutions have two major enemies: logic and common sense. Most of the world's great inventions were fathered by men with the ability to conduct their minds on free-wheeling adventures into the nonexistent, the unconventional, the absurd. Try it yourself on a problem you currently face. How might a child solve it? How would your wife tackle it? What would the ideal solution be? Suppose money were no object? What could you do if you had all the time in the world? Can you solve this in some combination? With what? With whom? Don't be afraid of getting wrong answers; you only need one correct one.

TRY THE OBVIOUS. A truck approached an underpass that was just one inch too low for it. Helpless, the driver pulled over to the side of the road. Presently, a little boy came by. "Truck too high?" he asked. "Yeah," said the driver. "Know what I'd do?" "What?" "I'd let some air out of the tires." All too often, the solution to a problem is right under our noses, hence out of sight. Answers that come immediately are not necessarily bad. An obvious road to a solution is to find out how others have handled the problem. Do some research at the library; in trade or professional journals; by writing to an appropriate governmental agency or business association; or by contacting an expert.

GET IT DOWN ON PAPER. Your pencil can be a helpful ally, too. Write out the problem as simply as you can. Study it. Jot down all the alternatives that occur to you, and if possible, draw pictures. Doodle. The mere act of *playing* with a problem sometimes yields the solution.

READ OUTSIDE YOUR OWN INTERESTS. Nothing will stimulate your "think muscle" like constant exposure to new and different ideas. So quite aside from the reading you do for strictly informational purposes and which has a direct bearing on the problem at hand, read books on history, economics, psychology, biography, science and travel. Study your daily newspaper, including the little out-of-the-way items. Subscribe to a magazine whose editorial policy is diametrically opposed to your own thinking. One paragraph, one sentence, even one word somewhere may suggest the solution you are seeking.

BRAINSTORM WITH OTHERS. Because ideas tend to generate more ideas, a noteworthy method of finding solutions is to talk over a problem with others: friends, colleagues, relatives—even children. Encourage them to give free rein to their imaginations and share their insights and inspirations, no matter how outlandish they may seem. Something that A says may trigger B who in turn may trigger C, and so on. Many ingenious ideas have been born through this kind of "free association."

4. SHAKE OFF IRRATIONAL THOUGHTS

Three common barriers to straight thinking threaten every potential problem solver. Unless you learn to recognize and hurdle these barriers, all the facts in the world will not do you a scintilla of good, for they distort the ability to reason and becloud perspective.

What are they?

(a) PREJUDICES. Customer Davis complains that you shipped him the wrong merchandise. You decide that Carter must be at fault; he was guilty last time. Your oldest subordinate can't possibly have anything worthwhile to contribute to your plan for improved quality control on the production line; he never studied engineering. Prejudice most frequently prevents one from viewing the unadorned facts of a case and causes one to reach irrational conclusions.

Take Carter. Simply because he was responsible for a past snafu is insufficient reason to judge him guilty now. On the contrary, having made a mistake once and "paid the price" of a dressing down, he may now actually be your most meticulous employee. Your senior subordinate's lack of formal engineering training doesn't *necessarily* prove that he is incapable of contributing good ideas for improving your production techniques. Indeed, his on-the-job experience may qualify him, on a practical level, as an expert.

No one is totally without prejudices. But recognize yours and you will have gone a long way toward eliminating the distortions of judgment that these prejudices can create.

(b) PRECONCEIVED NOTIONS. At one time or another, everyone "knew for a fact" that no Catholic could ever become President of the United States . . . space travel was a dream of science fiction writers . . . the sub-four-minute mile was beyond human reach. Yet, each of those "impossibilities" has materialized.

Why were so many people so dead wrong? Because they allowed preconceived notions to get between them and the facts; they carried conclusions in their heads that were arrived at *before* examining the evidence.

If you don't want to be the unwitting victim of preconceived notions, as you study the facts before you, ask yourself:

Am I assuming anything to be true here?

If so, do the facts bear out my assumption?

Are these "facts" demonstrable (e.g., via figures, current trends, past experience, written records, expert testimony)?

Am I letting wishful thinking influence my judgment?

Am I confusing coincidence or chance with cause and effect?

Do any of my interpretations of the facts fail the test of logic?

(c) EMOTIONS. Ask a young man in love how the weather is on a rainy day and he'll tell you, "Beautiful!" His judgment is untouched by the cold meteorological facts.

Similarly, *any* feeling—joy, hate, fear, suspicion, jealousy—interferes with the weighing of hard facts. The rule to remember and practice, therefore, is: *don't try to study the facts of a problem situation while under the influence of a strong emotion.* Rather, recognize your temporary inability to be objective and postpone your confrontation of them.

5. ARRIVE AT A TENTATIVE SOLUTION

Once you can clearly view the facts without distortion, you may reason your way through to a logical solution of your problem. Having satisfied yourself that you have obtained the pertinent facts of the case and successfully sidestepped the barriers to straight thinking in your assessment of them, you arrive at an answer that *appears* to be correct.

But is it? Really?

The most effective way to find out is to

6. TEST YOUR SOLUTION

Here are three practical ways to do just that:

(a) BE YOUR OWN HARSHEST CRITIC. When a scientist believes he has solved a problem or made a discovery, he doesn't pat himself on the back. On the contrary, he repeats his experiments, rechecks his notes, considers the possibility of an "X factor" being at work, invites his colleagues to prove him mistaken. In short, he tries his very best to knock his solution apart! Only after it has withstood every conceivable sort of critical examination will he formally announce his discovery. Do the same thing with *your* solution. Look for trouble. Examine it for pitfalls, inconsistencies, and contradictions. Dig for reasons why it won't work. Does it, for example, require too much time, money, personnel? Will it create problems of its own? Is it impractical for some reason? Answers to questions like these will indicate drawbacks, suggest possible modifications of your solution.

(b) GET OUTSIDE OPINIONS. Since no man can know everything from personal experience and since different men have had different experiences, it follows that the more men you ask for help, the deeper the well of experience from which you are drawing. Whatever your problem may be, the odds are overwhelming that somebody else has already faced it or a problem very much like it. Take advantage of that. Ask others for their candid opinions of your solution. Whom? Your superior, a friend, co-workers, or anyone whose judgment you respect and whose own past performance and background suggest that he is in a position to give you worthwhile advice.

(c) TRY OUT YOUR SOLUTION. A tentative solution to a problem is really a kind of decision and, you will recall, before any decision is implemented, it should be subjected to a trial run. Do you think your office might benefit from an expanded staff? Test that notion with some temporary help before hiring additional full-time employees. Considering a major capital outlay? How about leasing the equipment for a trial period first? Whenever possible, test your solution in a small way.

7. MODIFY YOUR SOLUTION AS NEEDED

If your tentative solution passes all three tests, you can probably put it into action with confidence. If it fails any of the tests, don't give up; you've merely uncovered another, lesser problem. Somewhere along the line, you overlooked a fact; or weighed one incorrectly; or failed to use it imaginatively; or allowed an irrational thought to cloud your vision. Very well, start from the beginning and work your way through the formula again:

1. Assemble the facts.
2. Weigh the facts.
3. Play with the facts.
4. Shake off irrational thoughts.
5. Arrive at a tentative solution.
6. Test your solution.
7. Modify your solution as needed.

That's the scientific way to solve a problem. And it's the way that works best.

But as effective as this method may be, there are times when every executive faces what appear to be insoluble, more personal dilemmas. They stubbornly resist attack and, in any confrontation, it is the man, not the problems, who comes off second best. Like some "Maginot Line" of the mind, they are immune to frontal assault. But, like the Maginot Line, they can frequently be outflanked and conquered.

Let us consider, then, the darker side of self-management and some of the things that can haunt the best of men.

Chapter Nine

Dealing with Frustration

Let's face it. Nobody is telling you anything new when he tells you that frustration is an integral part of your work. It comes regularly, frequently, inevitably.

There is a very good reason for this. By the very nature of his calling, with its diverse demands—information to be gathered and analyzed, decisions to be made, people to be dealt with, elusive factors to be identified and manipulated—the executive is fated to some setbacks. There never was, never will be a man in a position of responsibility who bats 1.000 all the time. He makes errors in judgment. He cannot always foresee all the ramifications of a course of action. And the law of averages virtually dictates that he will encounter some negative reactions to his leadership every working week.

Some grow discouraged and give up, for all practical purposes, whether they admit it or not. They "play it safe," never stick their necks out, never know the heady feeling of wrenching achievement from adversity. Others, however, react differently. They relish the temporary tension because they recognize it for the spur to accomplishment that it is. Like a knife that grows keener from being honed at a whetstone, they only improve as men and managers from their contact with problems.

Frustration results from the interaction of many factors, some from within the individual and some from without.

Throughout a man's life—at home, at play, at work—frustration arises when his problem-solving activities meet resistance or are faced with the possibility of failure.

Specifically, let's examine the most common on-the-job situations which tend to generate tensions and cause frustrations and see what can be done to reduce or eliminate them. Generally, the solution lies in a new and more emotionally mature attitude toward these daily problems.

COMPETITION WITHIN YOUR ORGANIZATION

Does it disturb you when you learn that another executive has been tapped for a promotion? Or, that the other fellow's idea has been adopted instead of your own? Or, that X's department has outproduced yours? Don't let it.

Rather, recognize that nobody always can be top man. Healthy competition within an organization is all to the good and is desirable as a means of keeping every man on his toes and doing his best. But to expect yourself to win all the promotions, out-think everybody else, and outproduce everyone all of the time is not only unrealistic; it is literally unhealthy. As long as you are doing the very best you can and winning your *share* of the laurels, this internal competition should not prove a source of frustration or tension.

If, by chance, you are *not* doing as well as you think you should, go into "executive session" with yourself and see if you can't snap out of your slump. Maybe you haven't thought out your problem. Perhaps there is someone who can help you. Possibly an objective reappraisal of your situation will set you on the right path.

OUTSIDE COMPETITION

The Acme Company lands the contract you feel you should have had. Consolidated is growing faster than your firm. General's latest annual report makes your company's earnings look modest by comparison. There is nothing intrinsically wrong with comparing your performance with those of outsiders, unless you find yourself suffering from defeatism as a result.

The competition is "outperforming" you? Very well! Turn the tables! "Outdeserve" them through better planning, better quality, better distribution or marketing ideas, better service, better thinking, better selling.

Some executives select a specific competitor and use it as a target for a time, competing with it at the production, advertising or selling levels. Just as a race horse will perform far better against other horses than against a stop watch, so does the firm whose sights are on the concrete achievements of a rival rather than an inanimate quota chart.

A word of warning: don't pick an unrealistic opponent. There is little sense of accomplishment if you narrow an enormous gap by two percent. Rather, pick a competitor who currently enjoys a moderate edge over you, one whom you have a chance to overtake within a reasonable period of time.

Such healthy competition can have a tonic effect by introducing a sense of fun and healthy challenge into everyone's daily job. There's nothing, after all, that says business must be grim 100 percent of the time.

THE PRESSURES OF TIME

One of the most serious frustrations that plagues executives is the problem of finding time to do all the things they are supposed to do: keep abreast of their field; help form policy; attend meetings; issue instructions; check on subordinates; write reports, memos, and correspondence; and, of course, *think*. Unless the executive finds a satisfactory solution to this problem, he will feel harassed, overburdened, confused, perplexed—in a word, frustrated.

There is only one solution: *organization* of time, through planning. Long-range planning will set up a program of accomplishment for a thirty-day or even a sixty-day period; short-range planning sets up a weekly schedule; night-before plan-

ning pinpoints specific tasks to be done (or started) on the
following day. Some concrete suggestions:

DISPOSE OF THE THINGS THAT CAN BE HANDLED PROMPTLY

The few projects that remain are not hard to cope with
then, if the pile of work no longer looks like a hopeless task to
tackle.

TAKE TIME TO COMMUNICATE

A little time invested in explaining something thoroughly
to those who may be involved with you in a project can save
endless hours later by preventing misunderstandings or fuzzy
instructions.

DON'T BANG YOUR HEAD AGAINST A BRICK WALL

If a problem has you momentarily stymied, put it aside and
come back to it when your mood and mind toward it have improved. Be careful, of course, not to postpone the task in-
definitely.

EXAMINE MISCELLANEOUS DUTIES PERIODICALLY

You may find that some of them are merely habit and can
no longer be defended as necessary. Habit and routine have an
unbelievable power to waste your time and energy.

FAILURE

Your pet project is canceled by the front office. Your million-
dollar idea doesn't pan out. A completed job doesn't much re-
semble the picture of perfection you've been carrying around
in your head. In one way or another, you've failed and you feel
resentful and frustrated.

What can you do to regain your emotional equilibrium?

You can, first of all, realize that failure is not the end of the world. Rather, it is a stern teacher from whom you can—indeed, must—learn.

Then you can study your failure to determine its cause. Was it a case of poor preparation? Insufficient data? Bad timing? Incomplete follow-through? Upon reflection, for example, you may find that your failure is traceable to jumping to conclusions, misinterpreting certain facts, relying too little (or too much) on others, or simple carelessness.

When you have satisfied yourself that you know all the reasons for failure, you are ready for the next step of making sure that the cause of your failure is not permitted to recur. If possible, set up a procedure or adopt a policy guaranteeing permanent elimination of the trouble. For instance, if you have found that the cause of your mistake was your taking action with too little available information, you can take steps to assure yourself of obtaining sufficient information in the future.

The important rule is *never ignore failure.* If you do, you are apt to repeat it. It is, in short, no crime to fail. The crime is not learning from failure and not improving thereby.

Want to turn your next "lemon" into lemonade? Try this program.

ACCEPT THE RESPONSIBILITY

During the Johnson Administration, Washington Democrats told a story of the confirmed Republican who dreamed of four beautiful girls. He was awakened by the chirping of birds and found four starlings perched outside his window. Looking at his newspaper, he noticed that it was April 4—the fourth day of the fourth month. It all had to be of some significance, he decided, and checked the day's horse races. Sure enough, in the fourth race, a horse named Henry IV was starting from post position four. Rushing to the track, he bet $400 on the horse and confidently watched the race.

The horse came in fourth.

"Damn this Administration anyway!" he muttered, tearing up his tickets.

True or not, that story points up the all-too-human tendency to blame others for our own mistakes. While comforting, of course, there is one thing wrong with this approach. By refusing to accept the responsibility for an error, you virtually assure yourself of repeating it. And there is no profit in that. So, *when you make a mistake, admit it.* That's crucial.

ASSESS THE DAMAGE

Before you can deal with a mistake intelligently, you must know how bad it is. Areas to investigate include:

(a) ITS IMPORTANCE. There is a world of difference between the sales manager who incorrectly estimates future sales of a product in his district and a vice president of sales who persuades his firm to retool and introduce a new product with no consumer appeal. The sales manager can always revise his figures or run a sales contest to boost his salesmen's performance. The vice president may be responsible for losing a great deal of money for his firm, forcing it to retrench, or even go out of business.

In determining the importance of a mistake, however, beware of *underestimating* or *overestimating* it. In the first case, you overlook or minimize its effects. In the second case, you conjure up visions of imminent ruin which are unwarranted by the facts.

(b) ITS COST. Obviously, there is no comparison between a $50 mistake and a $5,000 blunder. In estimating the cost of an error, however, remember to include the value of time lost, manpower wasted, tools and equipment used.

(c) ITS REPERCUSSIONS on you, your department, and your company. Does it upset deadlines, interfere with the work of others, or adversely affect the "big picture"?

DETERMINE THE CAUSE

Everything, from a sneeze to a snowstorm, has a cause. If you want to profit from your mistakes, you must find out *why* it happened. When you do, you can take appropriate steps to prevent those causes from building up again.

Determining the cause of a mistake takes some detective work. And, like a detective, you will have to do a certain amount of interrogating. Some questions you will have to ask, and answer, yourself; some, you will have to put to others. Here are the most important ones

(a) "WAS MY PLANNING BAD?" In attempting to discover *why* something went wrong, consider your planning. Did you allow yourself enough time? Did you have enough money? Did you have the kind and number of personnel required for the job? Did you use the right equipment? Did you use the right kind of material? Did you anticipate the bottlenecks that developed? Such self-interrogation will tell you whether or not the reason for your error was poor planning.

(b) "WAS MY TIMING BAD?" Frequently, mistakes are caused by *poor timing*, the launching of a plan or enterprise at the wrong day of the week, wrong week of the month, wrong month or season of the year. Consider your timing, then, in any "post-mortem" of a mistake.

(c) "WAS MY INFORMATION BAD?" In your search for the cause of your error, review the information upon which you acted. As things turned out, was any of it unreliable? Incomplete? Obsolete? If your answer to any of these questions is yes, you have your villain—or one of them. Next time, use other sources.

(d) "WAS ANYONE ELSE AT FAULT?" Sometimes, we *are* innocent. The seeds of the error in question have been sown by somebody else such as a lazy subordinate who took an ill-advised shortcut; a supplier who failed to meet a deadline; a co-worker who simply didn't pull his share of the load. Don't look for scapegoats, but, nevertheless, don't overlook the possibility that your error may be the result of someone else's carelessness.

(e) "WAS MY PLAN PROPERLY SUPERVISED?" Did you rely *too* much on others for the implementation of your plan? It's unrealistic to expect them to bring the same interest and enthusiasm as you would to your pet project.

The solution to this is adequate supervision, which doesn't mean hounding or subjecting others to a steady snowfall of memos or telephoning them a dozen times a day. It *does* mean making their jobs crystal clear to them in the first place; keeping yourself available for (and encouraging) questions; checking on progress at reasonable intervals; insuring that those working together cooperate fully with each other.

DISCUSS WITH OTHERS

So much for the questions you ought to ask yourself. There still remains the job of cross-examining those who were involved in the error. These may be employees, customers, clients, suppliers—anyone. Whoever they may be, ask:

(a) "WERE COMMUNICATIONS POOR?" Because *we* know what we mean, we frequently assume that our instructions to others are clear. Sometimes they aren't. We omit a vital step; leave too much to the imagination; expect others to be mind readers. That's why it pays to check on communications. *Was* your plan clear? Was there difficulty in getting additional information? Were you sometimes unavailable for questioning? Did you inadvertently give the impression that you didn't want to be bothered by "details"? Did you refuse advice? Were you stubborn or domineering?

(b) "WERE TOOLS OR EQUIPMENT BAD?" A conked-out car, truck, office machine, or power tool can sabotage the best-laid plans. Defective wiring, shattered glass, or improper lighting can set back any schedule. It has recently been estimated that the United States loses more than $8 billion *annually* from rust and corrosion alone! So in your examination of others, find out whether poor equipment was at the root of your failure.

(c) "DID THEY RUN INTO UNEXPECTED PROBLEMS?" We can't always anticipate the problems that crop up between our goals and us. If, for example, the success of your plan depends on a subordinate obtaining certain information from Mr. Brown and Mr. Brown is away on his annual vacation, obviously your plan is stymied for a while. No matter what the project in which you are engaged, a hundred unexpected things can go wrong. Frequently, others are reluctant to admit that they failed to foresee some eventuality; it's up to you to get them to give you the facts.

At this point, you should have a pretty fair notion of the cause of your mistake. You've done a lot of necessary spadework. Now, and only now, are you equipped to cash in on what you have learned.

PREPARE A NEW PLAN OF ACTION

Generally, the reason for a failure dictates the remedial action to be taken.

Communications were poor because you weren't always available to subordinates? Make sure they have access to you in the future.

Your planning was poor because you underestimated the amount of money needed? Next time, allow yourself a financial "cushion" above and beyond your estimate.

Before you prepare your new plan you should:

(a) SALVAGE WHAT YOU CAN. One mistake doesn't prove that the plan or program in which it occurred is a totally poor one. It simply indicates that somewhere along the line, you erred. Everything you did *prior* to what went wrong may be perfect. Everything you did *after* what went wrong may be beyond reproach. Therefore, review your project from beginning to end, isolating those steps, phases or portions that remain unaffected by the mistake. These can be used again—with increased confidence, for they have already been tested on the firing line and come through with flying colors.

(b) REVISE YOUR APPROACH. You have identified those portions of your idea, plan or project that appear to work; your job now becomes one of correcting the portions that do *not* work.

Search for new methods. A fresh approach may pop up during an idle conversation with a friend, from the pages of a newspaper, or out of your own imagination. Luckily, they are easier to summon once you can say to yourself, "This is what's wrong." And, at this point, you can. The general rule is to keep alert. Specifically, expose yourself to sources of new ideas, solutions and methods of colleagues, other people in your field, and the printed word.

Get them down on paper. No matter how wild a new method may seem, jot it down; you can always evaluate it later. Besides, even a zany idea may trigger a new, more practical train of thought. Toward this end, always carry a pen or pencil and a small notebook with you.

Assign new people to jobs. If your "cross-examination" uncovers an incompetent or inadequate worker among the personnel involved in a job, revision may be a simple matter of "bringing in some fresh blood." Sometimes, too, a mere rearrangement of assignments unleashes new thinking, uncorks old bottlenecks.

Brief new personnel. Update these new people by explaining to them the mistake that was made and what you have learned from it. That way, they will avoid repeating the error, be better able to pursue new directions.

(c) LOOK FOR "BUGS." Before acting on your revised plan, examine it carefully for flaws. Does this approach *really* avoid the consequences of the failure it is replacing? Why? May it result in a new setback of some kind? To the best of your knowledge, have you considered all factors? The extra time this detective work may take is added insurance that you are on the right track. By subjecting each alternative to such an examination, you should eventually be able to choose the one with the very best chance of working out.

Now that you have prepared a new plan of action, it only remains to

IMPLEMENT YOUR NEW PLAN

Everything you have done up to this point is, in a sense, prelude and it's now time to put your new plan of action into effect. Here are three activities in which you must finally engage if you are to extract the full measure of lemonade locked up in your "lemon."

(a) PREPARE A SCHEDULE. Now that you know what your new goal is, make sure you know when you may reasonably expect to reach it. Set a time, day or date for the completion of each element and do your best to adhere to it. By thus establishing a schedule, you create a kind of advance warning system that helps you spot mistakes before they occur. Should you find that a particular element in your new plan is taking much less or much more time than you allotted to it, you can check immediately to discover why. Perhaps someone isn't following instructions or maybe some mechanical failure is to blame. Alerted, you can nip error in the bud.

(b) START IT ROLLING. Dive in and get to work. Make all necessary phone calls. Tackle the paper work involved. Delegate whatever jobs must be farmed out. If your project requires it, get firm commitments from other people, other departments, other companies.

(c) FOLLOW UP. Essentially, this consists of two things:

Good communications. Are all written messages and instructions clear? Are lines of communications as uncluttered as possible? That is, can you reach others—and they, you—swiftly?

Are you all "speaking the same language"; or is technical jargon liable to interfere with true communications?

Keeping tabs on progress. Is everyone doing what he is supposed to? Are all the "gears" in your plan "meshing"? For example, if B cannot do his job until A completes a certain part of his, how is A coming along? Are those involved in the project cooperating with each other? How about yourself? Are you "on top" of the situation, in control of all elements? Are the people to whom you have delegated responsibility shouldering it in the manner you wish? Who needs help? And how can you help him? Is your schedule being followed? These questions are vital parts of any successful follow-up. If you can answer them satisfactorily, pat yourself on the back. You've earned it!

It would, of course, be a far easier world to live in if we never failed. But since we do err, success is apt to go to those who learn to turn their goofs into gold. The foregoing suggestions should, at the very least, put you on the right track.

A WORD ON TEMPER

Among the primary sources of executive frustration are imperfect subordinates.

It's a rare manager indeed who, at least once in a while, isn't firmly convinced that his department's performance would perk up dramatically if one employee or another were quietly throttled.

On a more realistic level, he settles for occasionally blowing his top or venting his emotions through thinly disguised sarcasm. The result is a sulking staff with drooping morale whose performance hits another low and a king-size headache for the executive.

CONTROL TEMPER

This is the easiest advice in the world to give, but among the hardest to take. How do you do it?

One way is to compel yourself to back off from the immediate situation and try to see it objectively, preferably in a larger context. So Miss Jones misplaced some important correspondence. Will empires fall? Is the few minutes' delay to find it really sufficient reason to ruin your day and digestion? Really?

Another technique is suggested by an incident in the life of John D. Rockefeller.

A top executive of the Standard Oil Company once made an error in judgment that cost his firm more than $2 million. Understandably, colleagues of Rockefeller decided to avoid their chief on the day he heard the news, lest they become the target of his wrath.

The exception was Edward T. Bedford, a Rockefeller partner. He entered Mr. Rockefeller's office prepared to listen to a long harangue against the offending executive, only to find the head of the Standard Oil empire busily writing at his desk.

After some minutes in which the only sound was the scratching of his pen, John D. Rockefeller looked up at his visitor.

"Oh, it's you, Bedford," he said calmly. "I suppose you've heard about our loss?"

Bedford nodded.

"I've been thinking it over," Rockefeller said, "and before I ask the man in to discuss the matter, I've been making some notes." He handed the sheet of paper on which he had been writing to his partner.

Bedford reported it this way:

"Across the top of the page was written, 'Points in favor of Mr. ———.' There followed a long list of the gentleman's virtues, including a brief description of how he had helped the firm make the *right* decision on three separate occasions that had earned many times the cost of his recent error.

"I never forgot that lesson. In later years, whenever I was tempted to rip into anyone, I forced myself first to sit down and thoughtfully compile as long a list of his good points as I possibly could. Invariably, by the time I finished my inventory, I would see the matter in its true perspective and keep my temper under control. There is no telling how many times this habit has prevented me from committing one of the costliest mistakes any executive can make—losing his temper.

"I commend it to anyone who must deal with people."

DISSATISFACTION WITH ONESELF

Who among us can honestly say he has fulfilled the ambitions of his youth? Precious few. The world is full of men who once dreamt of winning a Nobel Prize; writing a great novel; founding a business empire; teaching the world something new. Today, these same men may be found in our research laboratories, public relations firms, middle management, or universities.

Even the most mature may occasionally sigh at the discrepancy between the "private dream" and the "public reality." We may be congratulated by our peers, boosted by our families, promoted by our companies, respected by our communities, but still, in moments of reverie, remember the secret, unrealized pledges we once made to ourselves.

At times like these, current achievements may seem pale and insignificant. Dissatisfaction with ourselves sets in and we find ourselves "down in the dumps."

The solution? Take a long, hard look at the other side of the coin. Instead of dwelling on how far you have to go, consider how far you have come. Did you think, say ten years ago, that you would be earning the kind of money you earn today? Or shouldering the responsibilities you now carry? Probably not. How many people, directly or indirectly, completely or in part, rely on you for their own well-being? Doubtlessly more than you thought. How many people could do your work as well as you do it? Fewer than you imagine.

In short, accept the fact that *all* men, including you, have limitations. But don't dwell on your shortcomings.

But if those shortcomings continue to loom large in your mind, do something about them.

We are all probably guilty, to some extent, of allowing ourselves to get into a rut. If it isn't too deep, we can jump out. Too often, however, it takes some real pole vaulting to escape.

Here are six suggestions for adding some variety to your life.

1. CHANGE THE WAY YOU DO SOME PART OF YOUR JOB

And the more extreme the change, the better. Even so simple a variation as answering your own telephone can have ramifications. It will expose you to new people, new thoughts, new situations.

2. PARTICIPATE IN A DEMANDING OUTSIDE ACTIVITY

Take part in local politics, some voluntary organizational work, an evening course in some far-out subject you've always been interested in but never had time for, such as Renaissance art, the modern novel, archeology, or gardening. *Any* activity that compels you to break out of your own "vicious circle" can stimulate you and make you more interesting.

3. MAKE A NEW FRIEND

Go out of your way to meet new people. The neighbor you barely know may be in a fascinating line of work; the man you run into at a concert, church gathering, or civic affair might provide just the kind of mental stimulation you need. Or, call up an old acquaintance you've lost contact with. People change, develop, marry, go into interesting, offbeat businesses and professions. And don't be afraid of being rebuffed. Few things are more flattering to hear than, "I'd like to make your acquaintance" or "I'm looking forward to renewing our friendship."

4. VISIT A STRANGE PLACE

If you live in a large city, you've probably only scratched the surface of its possibilities. Ever witnessed a Chinese play? When was the last time you visited a planetarium? Have you ever attended an auction; seen how a large newspaper is printed; or eaten Javanese food? If you're a suburbanite, how about leaving the car behind and taking a long, leisurely walk to another neighborhood? You'll be surprised by what you'll see, whom you'll meet.

5. SET A LONG-RANGE GOAL

Most of us know what we'll be doing next month, even next year. But what about three, five, or ten years from now? Where do you want to be? What do you want to be doing? How much would you like to be earning? Try sitting down and actually figuring out where you're going and the "means of transportation."

6. BRAG A LITTLE

Let those closest to you in on your plans, even some of your dreams. It will add impetus to your resolution, force you to do the things you know you ought to do.

In short, the secret of getting out of a rut is to create your own excitement. This can take the form of people, places, ideas, or plans. It's up to you.

CRITICISM FROM OTHERS

Some executives are thin-skinned and oversensitive. Others are the victims of tactless, heavy-handed criticism from their superiors. Whatever the reason, the executive who allows criticism, implied or clearly stated, to get under his skin is headed for a fall. He feels rebuffed and unappreciated, goes into a sulk, takes it out on family and subordinates and soon finds himself as ineffective on the job as off. This is a frequent source of frustration and tension.

And because it is virtually universal, it deserves a chapter of its own.

Chapter Ten

Criticism—How to Take It

If you think about it, there are just two days on which the average person is free from criticism: on the day he is born and on the day he dies. And, one is tempted to observe, he only escapes on those occasions because of extenuating circumstances.

In between, he is apt to be the target of a ceaseless barrage of criticism—in rough chronological order—from parents, friends, teachers, sergeants, sweetheart, wife, employer, employees, and the Internal Revenue Service. His doctor tells him he's eating too much, his accountant informs him he's living too well, his mother-in-law intimates that he's not earning enough. Bus drivers shout that he's blocking the aisle, policemen lecture him on double parking and his kids deliver the coup de grace by reminding him that he lives on the far side of the "generation gap."

It's terrible.

Or is it?

Criticism comes to all of us and it comes readily, steadily, and inevitably. It comes when we know we deserve it and, frequently, it takes us by surprise. But it comes.

The question is, how should we handle it? Disregard it? Sometimes. Listen carefully? Yes. Learn from it? Always!

For criticism, like explanation or persuasion, is a form of

communication. And communication means that another person is sharing a thought with you.

That's always a possible avenue to new knowledge.

To get the most out of the remarks leveled at you by your very next critic, try this five-step program.

I.   TAME YOUR TEMPER

"The trouble with you, Ed, is that. . . ."

If Ed is like most of us, it is doubtful that he will ever really hear what follows that short preface. For almost immediately, all the defense mechanisms in his mind and body are activated. His heartbeat accelerates, his blood pressure rises, adrenalin is released throughout his system, and his breathing rate increases.

At the same time, Ed's brain races along at fantastic speed, producing any number of rationalizations, fantasies, excuses and counter-accusations designed to help him save face.

"Jack's always been jealous of my abilities."

"Here comes the buck-passing."

"He probably just got chewed out by his boss, so now it's my turn."

"I could wipe up the office with this clown if I wanted to."

"The Little Man has to show how big he is."

"The Mississippi River will dry up before you can ever tell *me* what my trouble is, stupid!"

And on and on and on.

The only way to counteract this all-too-human reaction to criticism is to consciously draw the reins on your temper. Resolve that no matter what your critic tells you, you will force yourself to remain calm.

It won't be easy, admittedly. At first there is no way you can control the way your body reacts to the stings or criticism; but with practice, as you learn to master your temper, you will find that you can at least reduce the physical thunder and lightning to a light drizzle.

II. LISTEN

Once you have your temper under control, you can expend your energy more purposefully.

Granted, Jack may not know what he's talking about, but the only way you can ever be sure is by absorbing and understanding what he's saying. That means just one thing, so far as criticism is concerned; namely, to listen—to *really* listen—to what he's saying. Here are four ways to perform this deceptively simple activity more effectively.

1. STRIVE FOR OBJECTIVITY

Listen in terms of *what*, not *whom*, your critic is attacking. If he's talking about the way you delegate authority, for example, concentrate *not* on your personality or ego, but rather on the weakness in discussion. By divorcing your personal feelings from the subject at hand, you will achieve objectivity, one of the prime requisites of true listening.

2. RECOGNIZE YOUR PREJUDICES

A major barrier to good listening is simple prejudice. Because you dislike the way a man dresses, votes, or parts his hair, you transfer your disapproval to what he is saying. You think, "Why pay any attention to him?"

Yet, a man who wears loud clothes *could* be a brilliant engineer. Because somebody blinks a lot, it doesn't necessarily follow that his thinking is impaired. A Socialist, Swede, or Seventh Day Adventist might be able to tell you a lot you don't know about the overseas markets for your product. In a nutshell: be sure to distinguish between the critic and his criticism.

Ideally, your listening should be totally free of prejudice, but since this is practically impossible, do the next best thing: recognize your prejudices and make a conscious effort to discount them in your evaluation of what your critic is saying.

3. BEWARE OF "TRIGGER WORDS"

First cousin to prejudiced listening is emotional listening which causes an irrational reaction to certain words that are loaded with special meaning for you.

For example, an employee says to you, "I was just discussing the new compensation plan with some of the men at the union hall." Immediately, you see red. "Those ingrates!" you think. "If they think they're going to bleed another red cent out of me!" While you're taking mental stock of what you consider union abuses, your subordinate has told you what was actually discussed. Maybe you listen to him; maybe you don't.

Certain words produce a kind of hysterical deafness in each of us. Some people automatically set their minds on disapproval when they hear *labor, union,* or *Democrat.* Others react just as strongly to *management, free enterprise,* or *Republican.* Similarly, certain words can summon instant approval: *love, kindness,* or *success.*

In any case, when "trigger words" are allowed to cast their spell, good judgment and reasonableness go out the window; only unstable emotions remain. And that's the end of effective listening.

Again, the only way to combat the effects of "trigger words" is to become consciously aware of them. The better you get to know the words that have "loaded" meanings for you, the less emotional static they'll create for you.

4. KEEP AN OPEN MIND

You don't care how much experience Joe Edwards has in leasing equipment; you've already drawn up the vacation schedule for this year; nothing Harry Gordon can tell you could possibly be of interest, since he never had a bright idea in his life.

Another important barrier to hearing what is really said—"case-is-closed listening," a predetermined refusal to hear something. You dismiss a criticism as irrelevant, unwarranted, or invalid before you even begin to listen.

Yet, Joe Edwards' experience with leasing might be invaluable to you. The few minutes involved in drawing up a new vacation schedule might be an excellent investment in employee morale. Even Harry Gordon could have a sudden, inspired insight from which you might profit.

All these things might happen *if* you would only listen; but instead, you don mental earmuffs. Your mind is made up in advance. You have the courage of your convictions, you tell yourself. Maybe you do. But you don't have all the facts.

Here is an appropriate story: When he was asked how he could bear to read all the many unflattering things written about him, Abraham Lincoln once explained, "As unreasonable as it may seem, I always think to myself, 'It is just possible that this man knows what he is talking about.' On that assumption, I see what I can learn from him." It's a rare, but wise, attitude to bring to any kind of criticism. In short, keep your mind open; and while it's open

III. CONSIDER THE SOURCE

Who is criticizing you? *What* are his qualifications? *Where* has he gotten his information? *Why* is he criticizing you?

Finding out the answers will help you evaluate your critic's motives and judge the validity of his comments. If his background or experience merit respect, then his criticism probably does, too. But if he is not qualified to judge your actions, don't take what he says too seriously.

Similarly, an examination of any vested interests he may have in criticizing you can tip you off to the seriousness of his censure. For example, is he passing the buck in order to save himself from criticism? Then discount what he says accordingly. Is he criticizing from a genuine impulse to help you improve your performance? Listen to him in the same spirit. Or is he criticizing merely to vent his rage or compensate for his own inadequacies? Don't pay too much attention.

But don't overlook the identity, credentials or motives of your critic when the time comes to

IV. EVALUATE

After he has had his say, weigh your critic's remarks; everything you hear, of course, cannot be taken on face value. Just as you read the printed word with a critical eye, so must you learn to listen to the spoken word with a critical ear. This is the time to test his case with the questions:

What was he actually criticizing?

What were the authorities for his statements?

Was he logical?

Were his examples one-sided?

Did he lump facts and opinions together?

Did he over-generalize?

Was his conclusion valid?

Was his criticism only negative in character, or did he make positive suggestions that you might be able to implement?

Will your performance be improved by following his advice?

If you notice any discrepancies, weaknesses, or non sequiturs in his thinking, bear them solidly in mind when you finally

V. ACT

Having taken the four preceding steps, you are now ready to do something about what you have heard. If you are convinced that the criticism is valid and useful, accept it and change your ways accordingly. You may congratulate yourself on having learned something.

But if you decide that it is invalid, extract whatever you can from it—even if it is only a more realistic assessment of the critic's character—and forget the rest. In short, view criticism for what it truly is: a challenge to your ability to change, improve, and grow.

And, on those rare occasions when your critics still manage to get you down, draw solace from the observation attributed to Mark Twain: "If criticism had any real power to destroy, the skunk would have been extinct long ago."

One thing is certain: you will never be beyond criticism. But you can minimize your exposure to it by concentrating your energies on activities designed to garner praise. Some of the most important of these activities are dealt with in the next chapter.

Chapter Eleven

How to Make Yourself Indispensable

What does it take these days to be considered absolutely essential in business? What are the unique qualities that mark a man not just "promising" but "productive"? More specifically, exactly what can a manager *do* to deserve recognition and reward?

There are probably as many answers to these questions as there are managers, for no two companies' problems, products, or personnel are precisely alike. Yet, by common consent, there are certain characteristics "winners" everywhere share.

This is not to say that you must do all these things in order to make your mark. But as opportunities present themselves, you cannot go wrong if you try to do as many of these things as possible.

LOOK FOR TROUBLE

No business is so problem-free that it can't benefit from a careful scrutiny of its methods. Consider the areas in which problems can occur: labor, management, production, credit, distribution, traffic, selling, and lots more.

In your very own department, on your very own job, things are probably not as perfect as they might be. And if you think they are—look again. Raise your sights. Refuse to be satisfied with "things-as-they-are." Search for better ways by asking yourself questions such as: "What can be done more efficiently?" "How is money being wasted?" "What takes too much time?" "Where can steps be saved?" "Is there a better sequence for performing this job?" "What can be eliminated, combined, simplified, standardized?" Cultivate the habit of "positive dissatisfaction" with your job, not for purposes of griping, but for improving results. It pays to look for trouble.

ACQUIRE ADDITIONAL SKILLS

No matter what image of yourself you want to create, regardless of who your superiors may be, you can only benefit from adding to your personal know-how. If you're in middle management, broaden your horizons—and executive potential—by studying those aspects of running a business which are unfamiliar to you: finance, planning, production, marketing, and the like. If you're in the shipping department, learn all you can about traffic management. If you're a draftsman, take courses in architecture or engineering. Whatever your job today, recognition and a better job wait for you tomorrow—if you will only prepare yourself.

BECOME AN EXPERT

Not every manager yearns to be a vice president; many people are perfectly content with the jobs they have. There's nothing wrong with that, certainly. But no matter what you are happiest doing, you can do it better and earn additional recognition also. A line supervisor, for example, can increase his knowledge of his product and the products of his company's competitors. He can acquaint himself more thoroughly with company policy, the history of his industry, the entire manufacturing process involved in his product, his firm's research program, its marketing operation, and its customers' problems. If you become an expert in your chosen field and share your knowledge willingly, your reputation, as well as your "indispensability," are bound to grow. For knowledge is not only power; it is also prestige, authority, and self-assurance.

The man who knows, and knows that he knows, has no hesitations or fears when confronted by a situation that he is equipped to meet. A TV repairman isn't the least bit afraid of attacking the maze of wires which discourages you—and me—from tinkering with the innards of our own television sets. Hundreds of feet above traffic, a window cleaner goes nonchalantly about a job that leaves other men breathless. A jet pilot hops behind a panel of intricate controls with a supreme confidence no layman can fathom.

Why? Because each of these men knows his job; that is, *what* to do, *how* to do it, *why* to do it.

Know your stuff. Know it inside out. Saturate yourself with it. There is nothing that will put the spring of confidence into your walk and into your performance like being sure that you definitely, concretely, and specifically know what you are doing.

What kinds of knowledge must the effective manager acquire? All kinds, to be sure—the more, the better—and here are some suggestions.

JOB KNOWLEDGE

This includes not only knowing your specific responsibilities (that goes without saying), but knowing whatever is to be known about fulfilling them more effectively. It requires continuous updating as to new techniques, new discoveries in your field, and new approaches and solutions to problems.

One simple example: the young are growing in numbers, and as they enter the labor market—bright, educated, looking for meaningful work—they are upsetting many long-cherished business beliefs. Which appeals are apt to be most persuasive to them at the recruitment stage? To what on-the-job motivations are they most likely to respond? What is their definition of "satisfying work"?

Nothing in an executive's past experience is geared to prepare him for dealing with the new generation. In order to get the answers he needs, the executive must keep up with the news; with what other companies are doing; and with what young people are thinking. And then he must be willing to learn and change with the times.

The manager seeking ways to boost his own productivity should also define in his own mind the extent of his responsibilities, as is discussed in Chapter Four. What must he—and he alone—do? What can he delegate? By eliminating the routine drudgery of his job, he frees himself for more important work —work he can do better with the time gained through ridding himself of the petty and bothersome details.

He must also keep on top of whatever technological advances are being made in his field, be they in research and development, production, distribution or marketing. There is no specific formula for reaching this goal; but what he needs is curiosity, to read, to attend conferences or colloquia when possible, and to continue communication with his peers and colleagues.

COMPANY KNOWLEDGE

One way to simultaneously grow more knowledgeable and cultivate a new sense of your own worth is to get a new appreciation of the worth of your institution. For perspective, the manager should be familiar with the history of his firm and its industry. How did it get where it is? For what innovations is it responsible? What does it contribute to society?

What about its products? What manufacturing processes do the raw materials go through? What inspection and quality control methods does your manufacturing plant utilize to assure product excellence? The answers to such questions are often revelations, even to top brass.

One of the very best ways to acquire this type of knowledge is to tour your company's factory. And even if you have seen your products made, it's a good idea to refresh your memory and enthusiasm by revisiting the factory from time to time.

PERSONNEL KNOWLEDGE

Doubtlessly, you already know the people immediately under you, but how well acquainted are you with the functions and personalities of other departments? Who is responsible for pricing? To whom can you turn for information on your firm's compensation policy? How can you quickly lay your hands on copies of your company's last half dozen ads? Who is the resident expert on foreign markets? Once you know who they are and what they do in your firm, you'd be amazed at how much you can learn from the people with whom you ordinarily don't come into contact.

KEEP GROWING

Business is certainly business; but it is not solely business. The men who reach the top are invariably men of wide-ranging interests and accomplishments; they are as much at home amid a group of university trustees as they are at an industrial conference.

The key to their success is continual personal growth. And the secret of such growth is being interested in things and people.

You know how it is with a child. Everything he sees is transformed into a question: "What's that?" "How does this work?" "Why are they doing such-and-such?" The world of the child is a world of wonder which stirs his curiosity and captures his interest. Because he is interested, he is fascinated and alive. This is also the mark of the growing adult.

You can keep your own personality alive and flourishing by creating for yourself a concrete plan to improve your mind and then working at it. Begin with a subject that interests you. It may be the internal combustion engine or the philosophy of Confucius; the ice cap at the North Pole or the life of Sergeant York; the effect of space travel on the central nervous system or the economy of early Mayan civilization. The subject may be incidental to—or entirely divorced from—your business; the important thing is that you come to life when you get into it.

Then set aside a definite time each day to read and study about it. Let nothing interfere with this. Do this regularly for a few weeks and you will soon not allow anything to stand in the way of it, for the deeper you delve, the more interested you will become. You will find yourself asking questions and seeking answers. You will discover that your subject inevitably leads to many other subjects. In the process, your horizons will expand and you will experience the pleasure of growing mentally. Others will doubtlessly recognize a new vitality in you. And you will develop into a man more worth knowing than ever.

SEEK RESPONSIBILITY

There is a breed of man who can smell responsibility coming in his direction before it turns the corner and dodges it with the artfulness of Red Grange shaking off a Michigan tackle. His greatest ambition in life is anonymity and he usually achieves it. There is another breed of man who welcomes the challenge of the big moments; who doesn't have to call a mass meeting every time he has to make a decision; who gets all the information he can, but then he says to himself, "Now it's up to me." A kind of extra muscle grows on such a man. He gets the self-starter's habit of action and command. He does not hesitate or procrastinate. He gets things done.

If you look around for something to do when your immediate assignment is fulfilled; if you stay with a job when others would let down; if you're willing to show someone else how to do something—you're the responsible kind who's likely to get noticed. If, on the other hand, you work *only* upon instructions and under supervision, you should turn over a new leaf. Immediately.

WORK HARD

Few things command more attention than old-fashioned hard work. Whether your particular "public" consists of top executives, customers, stockholders, or boards of directors, your diligence on the job will speak volumes in your favor. Demand—and get—that extra effort from yourself. Make it a standing rule to go "beyond the call of duty."

Writing a report? Make it the best report of your career! In charge of a project? Put in the few extra licks that can lift it out of the run-of-the-mill! Fighting a deadline? Beat it! The man who works hard every day is still rare enough to stand out in any crowd.

UPGRADE YOUR PERFORMANCE

Most of us tend to view our work, after a while, as routine; consequently, there is the ever-present danger of settling for routine performance. If you would like to upgrade the quality of your work, try this extraordinary experiment.

For two weeks, be a perfectionist. Take infinite pains with every detail of your job. Write letters over as many times as necessary to make them say precisely what you mean, no more, no less. Review and modify decisions until they appear flawless. Handle each task like a great artist putting the finishing touches on his masterpiece. Obviously, you are responsible for a certain volume of work and cannot be a driving perfectionist all the time, but the discipline of this two-week-long experiment will carry over to your future work and leave an indelible stamp of quality on it.

GET YOUR SUBORDINATES TO PRODUCE

To a large degree, your value to your firm hinges on the performance of those who work under you. If they get things done, you rightfully share in the overall accomplishment. If they do not produce, again you are rightfully held responsible. To get your subordinates working on all cylinders, try this program:

KNOW YOUR PEOPLE

The continuous study of "what makes them tick" is a must for getting things done through people. Human motives and attitudes are important clues for the executive and they can be determined only by careful scrutiny of every individual under you. Since security is the main drive in most people, giving recognition to the contribution of others and to their role in your company or department is a useful starting point in getting them to put forth their best efforts.

Of course, people vary widely in their other characteristics. Well-timed praise may spur one person to new heights of achievement, but it may only inflate another. The skillful executive constantly hunts for the right approach with each individual. For background, he searches beyond the office or plant. Since people's motives and attitudes are heavily conditioned by personal situations, a tactful drawing-out of subordinates can often supply invaluable information for understanding them.

SET A GOOD EXAMPLE

If you are irregular in your own work habits, late for appointments, fuzzy in expressing yourself, careless about facts, bored in attitude, the people under you probably will be, too. On the other hand, if you set and live up to a high standard yourself, in all probability they will be eager to follow your good example.

BE CONSIDERATE

Few things contribute more to building a hard-working team than a considerate chief. Be calm and courteous toward your subordinates. Consider the effects on them of any decisions you make. Take into account their problems, both business and personal. Do all you can to build up their pride in their work and their self-respect.

BE CONSISTENT

If you "fly off the handle," you are likely to frighten your people into their shells; if you vacillate wildly in reaction, mood and manner, you will probably bewilder them. Neither pattern of behavior will win you their confidence and cooperation, which you must have to get things done. People follow only that leader whose course is steady and whose actions are predictable.

EMPHASIZE SKILL, NOT RULES

Judge your subordinates' actions by their results in terms of increasing both the strength of your department and the satisfaction of the human needs of the people who work in it. Go easy on pat rules, for doing it "by the book" isn't always the most satisfactory way. If an unorthodox solution works effectively and pleases the people who use it, don't discount it just because it isn't "according to Hoyle."

LISTEN THOUGHTFULLY AND OBJECTIVELY

The boss who knows his people, their habits, worries, ambitions, and touchy points comes to appreciate why they behave as they do and what motives stir them. The best and fastest way to know them is to encourage them to talk freely, without fear of ridicule or disapproval. Try to understand how others actually feel on a subject and whether or not you feel the same way. Never dominate a conversation or meeting by doing all the talking yourself if you want to find out where your people stand.

GIVE OBJECTIVES

Your subordinates should have a sense of direction—know where they're going, what they're doing, and why they're doing it—in order to plan their time intelligently and work effectively. Good employees seldom enjoy working from day to day.

Therefore, make clear the relationship between their daily work and "the big picture"—the larger company objectives.

"DISGUISE" INSTRUCTIONS AS SUGGESTIONS OR REQUESTS

If your people have initiative and ability, you will get vastly better results in this way than you will by giving orders or commands. Issue the latter only as a last resort. If you find that you *have* to give orders all the time, you had better re-examine the way you have been handling your own job.

DELEGATE RESPONSIBILITY FOR DETAILS

You are not doing your real job as a boss if you do not delegate because if you insist on keeping your hand in details, you discourage your subordinates by competing with them. Moreover, by doing everything yourself, you prevent subordinates from learning to make their own decisions. Sooner or later, the capable ones will quit and the others will sit back and let you do all the work.

SHOW FAITH AND HIGH EXPECTATIONS

People tend to perform according to what is expected of them. If they know you have the confidence in them to expect a first-rate job, that's what they will usually try to give you.

KEEP SUBORDINATES INFORMED

Bring your people up-to-date constantly on new developments and let them know well in advance whenever changes are in the offing. As members of a team, they are entitled to know what's going on. Give them enough information about conditions and events in your company and industry to let them see themselves and their work in perspective.

ASK FOR COUNSEL AND HELP

By thus bringing your subordinates into the picture, you accomplish two important things: you give them a feeling of "belonging" and help to build up their self-esteem. As a result, they will be anxious to work harder than ever. What is just as important, they may well have good ideas which may never be utilized unless (a) you ask for them and (b) they are made to feel that you genuinely seek their help.

GIVE A COURTEOUS HEARING TO IDEAS

Many ideas may sound fantastic to you, but it's important not to act scornful or impatient. There is no surer way to discourage original thinking by a subordinate than to disparage or ridicule a suggestion he makes. His next inspiration might well be the very one you need, so make it easy for that next idea to come to you.

GIVE A CHANCE TO PARTICIPATE IN DECISIONS

When your people feel they have had a say in a decision, they are much more likely to go along with it. If they agree with the decision, they will look at it as their own and back it to the hilt. If they don't agree, they may still back it more strongly than otherwise because their point of view was given full and fair consideration.

TELL THE ORIGINATOR OF AN IDEA
WHAT ACTION WAS TAKEN AND WHY

If you do, he'll study other problems and make suggestions on ways to solve them. If his idea is accepted, he will be encouraged by seeing the results of his thinking put into effect. If his idea is not adopted, he will accept that fact more readily and with fuller understanding if you show him that the reasons for rejection are clear and sound. In addition, knowing exactly why his idea was impractical will help the suggester analyze the next problem more clearly.

BUILD UP SENSE OF WORK VALUE

Most people need to think their jobs are important. Many even have to feel that they not only have an important job but are essential in it, before they start clicking.

LET YOUR PEOPLE KNOW WHERE THEY STAND

The day of "treat 'em rough and tell 'em nothing" has passed. A system providing periodic ratings for employees is the first step. However, you will get full value out of such a system only if you discuss ratings with each person individually so that he can bolster weak points, clear up misunderstandings and recognize his particular strengths and talents.

CRITICIZE OR REPROVE IN PRIVATE

Reprimands in the presence of others cause humiliation and resentment instead of a desire to do better in the future. Criticizing a man in the presence of others undermines his morale, his self-confidence, and his desire to do his best for your company. So if you must criticize, keep it on a "man-to-man" basis, away from prying eyes and eager ears.

PRAISE IN PUBLIC

Most people thrive on appreciation. Praise before others often has a multiple impact. It tends to raise morale, increase prestige and strengthen self-confidence—important factors in the development of capable personnel. But be sure that those you praise are really the ones who deserve it and that you don't encourage "credit grabbing."

GIVE CREDIT WHERE DUE

Taking credit for what really belongs to one of your people tends to destroy his initiative and willingness to take responsibility. Giving him fair recognition for what he does has a double benefit: he gets appreciation for doing a good job, and you win the cooperation and support of a loyal worker.

In short, the secret of making yourself indispensable in business is really no secret at all. All it requires is imagination, initiative, a sensitivity to the needs of others, and plain old hard work. Perhaps the reason so few men are truly indispensable today is that those four qualities are not so common as we think.

Chapter Twelve

The Gentle Art of Tooting Your Own Horn

As good as you may be at your job and as hard as you may work at it, you may still go unnoticed by the people whose attention it is to your advantage to attract. The retirement rolls are filled with the names of people who did what was expected of them—and more—but who somehow never succeeded in rising above the crowd.

What they lacked wasn't the desire to succeed; nor the ability; nor, sometimes, even the opportunity. Their problem wasn't a failure of talent. It was a failure of imagination, an inability to call attention to their merits.

And yet, the world being what it is, we must often become our own publicists. It is only in bad movies that the hero, working as a singing waiter in a third-rate restaurant, is discovered by the world-renowned impresario and transformed overnight into the greatest tenor of all time. More realistically, we must contrive our own discovery by making sure that our good points are noticed by the people who are in a position to appreciate and help us cash in on them.

Understand that it is in no way bad taste, blameworthy, or immoral to call attention to your abilities and achievements. It is only the means you use that are open to scrutiny and judgment.

On the assumption, then, that you deserve recognition, here are the techniques that will help you get it.

SPEAK UP

It's the most direct way to bring your achievements—and your-self—to the attention of those whose esteem and approval you seek. Know a way to reduce costs? Tell your boss. Learning a special skill? Let your superior know. Landed a big account? Mention it to your next prospect.

There are at least four kinds of opportunities for "speaking up."

USE ORDINARY CONVERSATION

Information has a way of "percolating" upward and out. In your day-to-day contacts, you undoubtedly talk to *some* people who, in turn, pass along part of what you say in *their* day-to-day contacts. Since you never can tell where this "chain of talk" will end, forge as many "links" as possible. If, for example, you think you know how a time-consuming form can be restyled and streamlined, mention the fact to your colleagues, without going into details (after all, you want the credit for your idea). Sooner or later, the man to whom you report will say, "Tell me about your brainstorm." The opportunities for sowing these conversational seeds around are at lunch, during coffee breaks, traveling to and from work, and on the job.

BE CURIOUS

Every good idea is, at some stage, the result of one or more questions. Why are all reports filed in quadruplicate? What would happen if a certain process or procedure were done differently? Or eliminated altogether? Why is your product packaged the way it is? How can you help a customer solve some emergency? Before you can answer such questions, in all probability you will have to ask additional questions. Ask them! The act alone will point up your desire to find better ways. But bear in mind that questions should have a reason for being; do *not* ask them just for the sake of making an impression, lest you earn a reputation for being a pest or a "phony."

ADDRESS GROUPS

There is a continuing demand for knowledgeable guest speakers by a wide variety of organizations such as business clubs, professional societies, trade associations, fraternal groups, civic committees, and so on. If you have something of value or interest to say, or are an expert on a particular subject, here is a tailor-made audience for you. Let your availability be known by informing your boss or your company's public relations department; the officers of whatever organization you would like to address; members of various groups; friends; neighbors; relatives.

BY APPOINTMENT

There was a time when it was unthinkable for an employee, regardless of his title, to tell his superior what was on his mind. Fortunately, things have changed. Business and industry now recognize the importance of communications up as well as down the line. Consequently, most doors are kept open to employees. Particularly welcome in these days of tough competition, rising costs, and a tight labor market are ideas. If you have one that you think deserves serious consideration, ask for an appointment with the man in charge of the department or division involved. Almost certainly, you will get a cordial hearing, and recognition.

MAKE YOURSELF THE SUBJECT OF CONVERSATION

As old as gossip and as new as tomorrow's headlines, this technique enables you in effect to create a corps of publicity agents for yourself.

How can you get yourself talked about?

First, by talking to the "influentials" in your life, those people who, by virtue of their positions, authority, and contacts, can help you get noticed. They will vary according to your needs, but generally will include community leaders, your superiors, people who know your superiors, customers or clients, and so on. Have an idea for a civic project? Talk it over with your local banker. Got a pet peeve? Tell the editor of your hometown newspaper. Know how to increase good will for your firm? Mention it to your boss. Things get around.

Second, invite recommendations and testimonials to your abilities. Thus, a customer was delighted with the machinery a certain company had tailored to his specific needs. He telephoned the firm's production manager and told him so in glowing terms.

When he was through, the production manager said: "I appreciate this very much and all I can say is that I was glad to be able to do what I did do. But I'd like to make a suggestion. You can help me a lot if you put this in a letter and send it to my boss." The customer took the hint and put his praise in writing.

"That letter of commendation," reports the production manager, "was read not only by my superior, but was passed around the office. It gave me a big boost."

Next time somebody of importance compliments you on something you've done, suggest he pass the word along where it will do you additional good. Asked in the right way, most people enjoy doing favors for others.

Finally, don't be afraid to take sides on controversial issues. This doesn't mean that you ought to involve yourself in office politics, petty feuds, or tinderbox issues like religion. It does mean that you ought to think through and form opinions on issues that affect you as an employee and a citizen. Today when companies are growing more aware of their social responsibilities, such employee involvement is generally encouraged. If your industry finds itself in the middle of the pollution problem and you have strong feelings on the matter, get them off your chest. If you approve of your company's hiring policy toward minority groups, go on record as favoring it. If you're against the new reorganization plan, articulate your arguments. The City Council doing something you don't like? Discuss it with friends and neighbors. Once you get yourself identified with a particular cause or point of view, your name will tend to come up when that cause or point of view is discussed by others.

DON'T OVERLOOK THE POWER OF THE PEN

Bob Peterson is now the chief engineer for a tool manufacturer, but ten years ago he was just another supervisor on the plant floor. How did he get ahead? There is no one answer to that question, of course, because Bob was always ambitious, worked hard, put in overtime, took evening courses to help him increase his value to the company. But one of the things he did regularly was bombard management with ideas via the company suggestion program. So often did he work into the early morning hours dreaming up his ideas and getting them down on paper that his wife jokingly suggested, "Why don't you get a rubber stamp?"

And he did! For a few dollars, he had a rubber stamp prepared in bold type that read: **Another idea from Robert Peterson!** From that moment on, every single one of his suggestions bore that familiar legend. It wasn't long before he was tapped for advancement. The moral is clear: the written word is still a first-class ticket to recognition.

Here are five ways to harness the power of the pen on your own behalf.

THE COMPANY SUGGESTION BOX

Take a tip from Bob Peterson. Just about every firm runs a suggestion program and rewards good ideas. Think of some, write them up, sign them plainly, and get them on their way. Make them as good as you can and don't rest on your laurels.

MEMOS

A good idea frequently requires detailed explanation or is meant for the eyes of just one man. In such cases, draw up a memo of two or three pages on the subject, explaining what the problem is, your solution to it, why you think it will work and submit it through the proper channels.

COMPANY PUBLICATIONS

Many firms publish one or more newspapers or magazines for internal circulation. The editors of these "house organs" are at least as interested in getting news as you are in getting noticed. And they are particularly interested in success stories that may inspire others. Hence, you can feel free to "toot your own horn." Some suggestions for items: the establishment of some kind of record (number of products shipped, sales made, units produced, amount of material handled); a promotion; the winning of an award, not necessarily connected with your job; your part in landing a big contract or account; participation in a company-sponsored social or civic event. Don't think that you must be a Hemingway in order to submit a news item. Just write down the facts; the editor will glady whip them into shape.

BUSINESS AND TRADE PRESS

Actual Specifying Engineer, Building Supply News, Ceramic Industry, Design News, Electric Light & Power, and *Farm Equipment* are just a few of the more than 2,000 trade, technical, and professional magazines that roll off the presses every month. Almost certainly, there are several specialized publications in your own field that would welcome a contribution from you. If you've solved a technical problem; discovered a new management technique; developed a new inventory method; made your plant, office, or store more efficient; discovered a way to increase profits or cut costs; enlarged your business; tapped a new market for your products or services— write it up in article form, take a few pictures to illustrate it if possible and send it to the editor. Your by-line over an article in a trade publication will be seen by precisely the people whose notice you are seeking—those in your own field, including personnel of your own firm.

LETTERS

Whether it's a thank-you note to a good customer or a hard-hitting "beef" to some editor, letters can be attention-getters, too. There are literally hundreds of occasions for sitting down at a typewriter or dictating a brief message such as: congratulate someone on a job well done, a promotion, any achievement of which he is proud; pass along news or ideas; ask for information or advice (thereby transforming the recipient into an "expert"); seek an appointment to discuss some matter of mutual advantage; go on record as approving or disapproving some contemplated course of action; take a "survey" on a subject dear to the heart of the man to whom you are writing; comment on trends in your company or industry.

PARTICIPATE

Taking part in various kinds of activities is still another way of becoming a familiar figure in those circles interested in what you are doing. A few tips:

GET IN ON COMPANY OR INDUSTRY PROJECTS

Consider the opportunities within your own field or firm. Projects like trade shows, publicity campaigns, conventions, symposia, "open house" activities require volunteers. Be one! One thing frequently leads to another.

BE A JOINER

Your local Chamber of Commerce, trade or business association will welcome you with open arms, for it wants as many members as it can get. As your reward, you will mingle with the people in the "next higher echelon," meet them on a personal level which is often difficult, if not impossible, within the stratified business world. It's a golden opportunity to make contacts and get known. People whom you might never be able to meet in any other way could very well be fellow joiners.

VOLUNTEER YOUR SERVICES

As a Boy Scout leader. As an unpaid fireman. As an amateur actor. As head of a church bazaar. As a member of a charity drive. The possibilities, like the ramifications, are virtually endless.

GET APPOINTED TO COMMITTEES

People are notoriously shy about assuming positions of responsibility and reluctant to get involved in new undertakings. You can be different, when and where it counts, by letting it be known that you are interested in helping get things done.

Whether or not you agree with Oscar Wilde, who said, "The only thing worse than being talked about is *not* being talked about," one thing is clear: it is usually the people whose names you hear on others' tongues who get ahead in this world. And most often, they themselves are responsible for the publicity. Or, to put it more memorably, consider this anonymous observation:

> *The codfish lays ten thousand eggs,*
> *The homely hen lays one.*
> *The codfish never cackles*
> *To tell you what she's done—*
> *And so we scorn the codfish*
> *While the humble hen we prize.*
> *It only goes to show you*
> *That it pays to advertise!*

Chapter Thirteen

℞ for More Effective Writing

While the pen, as we have seen, can be an important means of self-promotion, it is also a vital part of an executive's daily life, for regardless of your specific responsibilities, the odds are that a significant part of your job revolves about expressing yourself on paper.

But do your letters, memos, and reports mean business? Or do they more often stand for fuzzy thinking, tough reading and fumbled opportunities? Here's a simple test to find out how your business writing rates. During the last month,

1. Did you have to write any additional letters or memos to explain what you meant in your initial communication?
2. Did you receive any telephone calls or letters from puzzled recipients, asking for clarification of your message?
3. Did you reread any of your own correspondence and wonder what on earth you were talking about?
4. Did you start a letter more than once, only to find that you still weren't really saying what you wanted to say?

If your answer to any of these questions is a sheepish yes, you can profit from what you are about to learn. Even if you can honestly say no to all four questions, you can doubtlessly improve your present writing ability by mastering a few simple principles.

Why should you ,other? Because, with the steady expansion of our economy, your own business horizons widen. With the development of new methods, new markets, new customers, and the growing trend among companies to disperse their operations,_there is a commensurately growing need for effective long-distance communications—and communicators. All things being equal, the out-of-town customer is apt to favor the supplier who is most persuasive on paper. In your own firm, if the fellow next to you writes better reports than you, chances are that his name is better known "up front" than yours

Remember—to many of the people with whom you deal, your letters *are* you. They've never seen you. They've never shaken your hand. They may never have spoken to you. The only way they have of sizing you up is through the words you put on paper. The right words, strung together correctly, sell you. The wrong words have the opposite effect.

Well-written business letters are efficient, too. They help you and those who depend on you get things done. Just as you wouldn't long tolerate a worker who dressed shabbily, made costly mistakes, and insulted customers, you shouldn't settle for less-than-effective business correspondence.

Finally, the letters you write cost money. It has recently been estimated that, including labor, materials and time, the "price" of the average business letter has passed the three-dollar mark and is inching inexorably upward. Why not get your money's worth?

Writing effectively isn't all that difficult. But before we get into the "do's," it might be worthwhile to examine

THE TEN DON'TS OF GOOD BUSINESS WRITING

Not necessarily in the order of importance, they are:

1. DON'T PONTIFICATE

You aren't a king, so don't be "we" unless you are speaking for your company. Don't "state"; you aren't handing down a Supreme Court decision. Don't tell somebody his letter is "in your hands" or "on your desk," or "before you." He doesn't care where it is as long as you've read it and he does want you to "read," not "duly note" it. Remember, a letter is a letter, not a "communication" and a date is a date, not an "instant."

2. DON'T TIGHTEN UP

Stiffness is all right in an upper lip or in a backbone, but in a letter it makes your words read like a picket fence. Be relaxed when you write and don't try to translate your thoughts into strange, unusual words that are completely foreign to the way you ordinarily say things.

3. DON'T SEND A CROSSWORD PUZZLE

He is not interested in solving a cryptogram. To organize your material, keep in mind that a letter or a report has a beginning, a middle, and an end; it is up to you to put the right things in the right place.

4. DON'T BE LONG-WINDED

Keep your story short and say what you have to say once. If you've said it effectively, once should be enough.

5. DON'T WRITE DOWN

You aren't teaching school and your reader is not inferior or necessarily ignorant. The condescending person is never liked and the condescending letter or memo is hardly likely to win friends or influence people.

6. DON'T BE A BULLY

Never get tough in a letter. Spoken words vanish into the air, but when you put them down on paper they stick around longer than a thirty-year mortgage, always ready to jump out of somebody's file to refute your claim that you were misquoted or misunderstood. Corollary: never write a letter in anger. If you must, get it off your chest, then tear it up.

7. DON'T BE RUDE

Abrupt, curt letters are annoying even though the writer may not have intended to be discourteous. Always read your letters over before you mail them, therefore, and try to put yourself in the place of the recipient by asking, "How would I like it if I got a letter like this?"

8. DON'T ATTEMPT TO BE TOO LITERARY

You are writing a business communication, not a sonnet. If you are a good craftsman, your letters will show that you have imagination, wit and intelligence, but there is no need to try for the grand style in prose. The final destination of your letter, after it gets past the reader, is his filing cabinet or waste-basket, not an anthology.

9. DON'T CLIMB A PLATFORM

You are writing a letter, not preaching a sermon or arguing from a soapbox. You want the reader to meet your mind, not study your ultimatums. Keep away from such phrases as "We insist," "Unless we hear from you," "You are put on notice."

10. DON'T WRITE IN A HURRY

Good writing takes time and thought. There are tricks to the trade and you learn them by practice. If you have ideas, an interest in your reader, a normal curiosity about language and the willingness to broaden your background through good reading, you can equip yourself to write.

Which brings us to the simple rules for effective business writing.

KNOW WHAT YOU WANT TO SAY

Sound obvious? It is! Yet, haven't you yourself received letters that go on and on, forever circling their subject but never really "zeroing in" on it? Take the following example, a reply to a prospect's inquiry:

> Dear Mr. Jones:
> We have been supplying envelopes to some of this city's biggest firms for over twenty-five years. We have all sizes and shapes. Our price list is enclosed. We've never had any serious complaints about our service and look forward to doing business with you. Thanks for contacting us.
> Very truly yours,

A bit vague? Certainly. No mention of delivery dates. Not a hint of any real interest in the prospect's needs. The "thank-you" is tacked on to the very end of the letter, like an afterthought. And there is even the uncalled-for admission that this firm's customers sometimes have reason to complain!

The writer simply did not think through what he wished to say. If he had, he might have written this letter:

> Dear Mr. Jones:
> Thank you for your inquiry of April 10, regarding our line of business envelopes.
> From your description of your needs, we think that any of the accompanying samples should fill your requirements, although I personally favor sample C for its simplicity and dignity. You will agree, I think, that your company's image can only be enhanced by top quality stationery. Should you wish additional samples, please let me know.
> You will find a complete description of our quantity rates

on the enclosed card. Delivery ordinarily takes ten days for quantities up to 100,000, a few days longer for more.

We'll get to work promptly upon receipt of your instructions.

Thank you again for getting in touch with us. We look forward to adding your name to our growing list of companies that we are proud to serve.

Sincerely,

Here is a logical, informative, polite letter of acknowledgment that also does a sound job of selling. It starts off by immediately recalling the letter to which it is a reply, goes on to show that the writer has given thought to Mr. Jones' particular requirements, gives the hard details (samples, prices, delivery) briefly and winds up with a subtle sales pitch. Mr. Jones is bound to be impressed and to give serious consideration to doing business with the writer.

The first, unbreakable rule of effective business writing, then, is *know what you want to say*. If necessary, make notes first. By thus arranging your thoughts on paper, in order of importance, you are actually organizing your letter, memo, or report.

USE THE "YOU" APPROACH

Psychologists have estimated that we spend fully 92 percent of our "thinking time" thinking about *ourselves*. This is neither praiseworthy nor reprehensible. It is simply an inescapable fact of life.

Very well. Put this fact to work for you in your business correspondence. Spotlight your reader's wants, needs, interests, and desires. Nothing, but nothing, is so geared to rivet his attention on what you are telling him as this "you" approach.

DON'T SAY: "Here is a new production technique that is being adopted by a lot of manufacturing firms."

DO SAY: "If you are like most production men, you will be interested in this brand new way of lowering your manufacturing costs."

DON'T SAY: "The enclosed brochure contains our whole story."

DO SAY: "You will find more than 100 new products described in the enclosed brochure."

DON'T SAY: "It is hoped that the foregoing answers the questions raised."

DO SAY: "Should you have any further questions, I would be happy to answer them."

Usually, it is a simple matter of "translating" the "I," "me," or "our" approach into "you" terms. Obviously, it is not possible to eliminate entirely the words *I* or *me* from a business letter. Nor is it desirable. It is just a matter of emphasis. As a rule of thumb, think in terms of the reader's self-interest and the "you" appoach will take care of itself.

BE CLEAR

Unless your letters, memos, and reports say exactly what you want them to say—no more, no less—they are apt to become trouble-makers instead of business tools.

Your job, therefore, is to make them crystal clear. Here are five ways to do just that.

1. BE BRIEF

Say only as much as you must to express your ideas without being curt. If you can explain an error in just three sentences, use three sentences. Don't worry about all the blank space that is left on the paper. The busy reader appreciates brevity.

2. USE SHORT WORDS AND SENTENCES

Test after test indicates that this improves comprehension. This isn't to say that your letter must sound like a kindergarten primer. It means that whenever you can substitute a short word for a long one, do so. It will only improve your "Clarity Quotient."

"Clarity Quotient"? That's a method of expressing the fog factor in writing. Language experts have devised several ways of measuring the relative clarity of a written message, but this simple three-step formula is one of the best:

(a) Count the words on an average page of your writing. Divide them by the number of sentences to get the average sentence length.
(b) Count the words of three or more syllables per 100 words.
(c) Add the two figures and multiply by 0.4.

The answer is your "Clarity Quotient." According to extensive tests, a Clarity Quotient above twelve is difficult reading. Above seventeen, a written communication requires the reading skill of a college graduate. Go much higher than that and your reader is apt either to misunderstand you or give up on your message.

Check your next piece of writing for clarity. Don't let a good idea get lost in a forest of gobbledygook.

P.S. The above discussion of the "Clarity Quotient" has a C.Q. of about nine.

3. LIMIT SENTENCES TO ONE IDEA EACH

Instead of creating a grammatical monstrosity like, "We are not interested in your new machine because the last one we bought from you has been giving us trouble and maintenance costs are far beyond our estimates," break it down with periods: "We are not interested in your new machine. The last one we bought from you has been giving us trouble. Maintenance costs. . . ."

4. BE INFORMAL

Except for relatively rare occasions, such as when you are writing to a president of a firm or a distinguished citizen, strive for informality. Short sentences are a beginning; it's hard to make a long sentence flow. Another serviceable technique is to vary punctuation. Do your letters, memos, and reports show that you're familiar with the hyphen? The colon or semicolon? The question mark? The exclamation mark?

5. BE SPECIFIC

Name names. Cite figures. Pinpoint dates. Give facts. If you must generalize, illustrate with concrete examples.

BE FORCEFUL

While clarity of expression is essential to an effective communication, it is not enough. You can write a letter to a girl telling her you love her. She may understand you perfectly. But will she answer you, see you, or reciprocate your affection? That's the final test of your letter.

That's what's meant by forcefulness. Virtually everything you write on the job is designed to elicit some kind of active response from the reader—even if it's only an emotional response, such as liking you. If your communications lack force, they'll get no response.

How, precisely, do you create force?

The first step is to decide exactly what response you want. Ask yourself: "What am I trying to get this guy to do?" When you've done this, you've built the backbone of your letter or report.

Second, write a rough draft. Start with an opening "hook" that will catch your reader's interest. Some suggestions:

PROMISE SOMETHING OF VALUE

"This memo will describe a method of reducing our truck downtime by 33 percent."

USE SUBTLE FLATTERY

"I'd like to ask your help with a difficult problem."

AROUSE CURIOSITY

"Our investigation has uncovered three areas where substantial savings can be made."

CHALLENGE THE READER

"When was the last time you figured out your net worth?"

Bearing in mind the action you're going to ask for at the end of your communication, drive straight toward it from this point on. This is the place to marshal your facts, figures, and arguments. Don't include anything that does *not* lead to your request for action.

Now write the last sentence or, in the case of a report, the conclusion or summary. Ask yourself how you want the reader to feel when he finishes. Impatient to get going on your project? Eager to meet you? Interested in hearing more? Get it into your concluding words.

WRITE THE WAY YOU TALK

For some strange reason, many ordinarily articulate people "freeze" at the sight of a blank piece of paper. The results are trite, pompous documents that accomplish little. Long words, mossy phrases, tangled sentences, and the disastrous notion that there is a special "written English" all conspire to defeat the prime purpose of a letter—*communication*.

The best antidote is to *write as you talk*. Some tips:

STICK TO THE ACTIVE VOICE

Say, "I've examined the proposed plant site," not "the proposed plant site has been examined"; "I appreciate your comments," not "your comments are appreciated." The active voice is dynamic, easily understood; the passive voice is wishy-washy and occasionally confusing.

USE COLLOQUIALISMS—EVEN SLANG

If good usage is the "meat-and-potatoes" of our language, colloquialisms and slang are its "salt and pepper." There are no real substitutes for such expressions as "cinch," "you bet," "bark up the wrong tree," and so on. But, like salt and pepper, they should be used sparingly for maximum effect.

BREAK THE "RULES," IF NECESSARY

English is a living, changing language. What was unacceptable twenty years ago may be fine today. Thus, you were probably taught in school that it's wrong to end a sentence with a preposition. Yet, there are times when any other construction sounds awkward. (Sir Winston Churchill buried this notion forever when he quipped, "This is the sort of arrant pedantry up with which I will not put!")

ABBREVIATE WHEN APPROPRIATE

Instead of writing, "I would not," for example, write "I wouldn't"—just as you'd say it.

BE MODERN

Avoid stuffy phrases like "please be advised" or "reference is made to yours of the 15th." Instead, use clear, concise language. For example,

Don't Say	*Do Say*
at an early date	soon
with your kind permission	if it's all right with you
enclosed please find	here's
acknowledge receipt of	received
am pleased to advise	I'm happy to say
regret to advise	unfortunately
you may rest assured	you can be sure
pursuant to our conversation	as we agreed; as you requested; as I said

An easy way to check a business letter or memo for pomposity is to read it aloud. Does it *sound* like you? If it does, you can be sure it reads well. If it doesn't, try again.

THE RIGHT WAY TO ANSWER A BUSINESS LETTER

Of course, you aren't always the initiator of a letter. Frequently, you are called upon to answer a letter written by somebody else. The vast majority of such business reply letters are deadly dull, cliché-ridden affairs that usually fail to do what they ought to do—answer another human being. Here are ways to improve your own written replies:

READ CORRESPONDENT'S LETTER CAREFULLY

Study it. If necessary, note important points in the margin. What, *precisely*, does he want from you? Information? Clarification? Instructions? An opinion? If he is seeking information, don't give him an opinion. If he is asking for an opinion, *don't* send him instructions. Common sense? Sure. But you would be amazed how few people bother to *read carefully* the letters they must answer. Result: prolonged correspondence, wasted time, and irritation for all concerned.

WRITE A FRIENDLY LETTER

Your major stock in trade is friendliness. Try to make this attitude apparent in your reply. As you write, think of the recipient as a friend. This attitude creates a better impression with your reader and, most important of all, places him in a receptive frame of mind.

DECIDE ON MAJOR THEME

Unless your correspondent is an old acquaintance, he won't particularly be interested in an over-long chatty letter. Stick to the point. The best business letter is one that is developed along one major theme. Once you decide on your keynote idea, visualize how you will deliver it to your reader so that he will agree with you. One effective method of doing this is to put yourself in his shoes, then ask yourself, "What benefit do *I* get out of it?"

COLLECT DATA

This information should bolster your theme, be pertinent to the matter at hand, prove your case. Remember—anything that distracts your reader works against you. We all have only a limited amount of mental power available at any given moment and our brains can only deal effectively with one matter at a time.

WRITE IT

Few things are more annoying than waiting for a reply to a letter. Therefore, unless special circumstances dictate otherwise (e.g., you must receive information from someone else before you can frame your letter), try to answer a business letter within forty-eight hours. It not only makes a good impression on the recipient; it keeps your desk cleared for action.

Following these common-sense rules won't turn you into a Shakespeare, obviously. But, followed diligently, they will help you write the kind of business letters, memos and reports that evoke the response in your readers that you want.

That's really all any business writer has a right to expect.

Chapter Fourteen

Potpourri: Tips, Tricks, and Assorted Techniques

Not every self-management technique deserves a chapter of its own. Some stand by themselves, little solitary gems of know-how without a setting in which to sparkle. Others seem especially designed to prod, provoke or merely point the way to self-improvement, leaving the details to individual development. Still others are so downright ingenious and offbeat that it would be unforgivable to omit them from a book like this. All have one thing in common: they are so good that they merit being brought to the attention of every executive seriously concerned with upgrading his performance.

Here, then, is a brief look at some of the less-traveled roads to better self-management.

PRACTICE BAD HABITS—TO BREAK THEM!

Finger drumming, chain smoking, knuckle cracking are just a few of the many habits that can annoy others, harm your "public relations." Most of us would confess to at least one bad habit that we would like to get rid of—usually "tomorrow." But why wait?

There *is* a little-known way to break a habit that appears to work for the vast majority of people. It may work for you.

Discovered by psychologist Knight Dunlap and dubbed the "theory of negative practice," it is simply this: *perform the bad habit consciously.*

Dr. Dunlap challenged the old idea that repetition can only entrench a habit more deeply. By consciously performing the habit, he reasoned, it might be possible to bring under *voluntary* control behavior which has been involuntary.

He experimented on himself first. He had long had the annoying habit of typing *hte* for *the* when striking his typewriter keys rapidly. In order to rid himself of the habit, he purposely typed *hte* several hundred times, all the while telling himself that he would *not* do it that way in the future. And it worked! He never made that mistake again. Further experiments, on people who stammered, for example, confirmed his theory.

Suppose you become aware that you have a habit of tapping your foot when socially uneasy. When you're alone, according to the theory, tap your foot while telling yourself, "I'm tapping my foot. I do it because I'm nervous and it shows everyone that I'm nervous. It's a pointless thing to do and I'm going to stop."

Note: Tests show that fifteen minutes of practice twice a day for several weeks produce best results.

FOR A MORE RETENTIVE MEMORY

If, like most people, your "forgettery" is better than your memory, you can probably profit from the results of recent research in the art of recall. Whether it's important to you to remember names, dates, telephone numbers, facts or figures, the following tips can help you do a better job.

INTEND TO REMEMBER

The memory is like a computer. It needs concrete instructions. Thus, to remember a man's name, "program" your memory. Don't merely listen as he is introduced. Deliberately instruct your brain: "I must remember that this tall, thin fellow with the mustache is named Ed Booth."

BECOME GENUINELY INTERESTED

No boy really enthralled by baseball has trouble memorizing all the players' batting averages. So "sell" yourself on the importance *to you* of the information you want to remember— and watch it soak in! If necessary, occasionally remind yourself of the advantages of remembering it.

USE AS MANY SENSES AS POSSIBLE

For example, if you want to memorize the opening paragraphs of a speech you are to give, recite them aloud. You will be using your senses of sight and hearing, which reinforce each other.

MAKE ASSOCIATIONS WITH KNOWN FACTS

Every fact you already possess is a "hook" on which you can hang some new fact. For instance, if you know what Italy looks like on a map, you can remember the location of Sicily by picturing it as being kicked by the boot of Italy.

INVENT YOUR OWN ASSOCIATIONS

The more bizarre, the better. If you want to memorize the Gettysburg Address and the first letter of each sentence forms a code for you, fine. If you can compose a nonsense rhyme incorporating a telephone number you wish to remember, then do so.

HOW TO PREPARE A SPEECH

Whether it's to address the next convention you attend or to kick off a community drive, your chances of being tapped to give a speech this year are very good. Of course, you'll want to give the best possible account of yourself. Some tips on putting your speech together:

KNOW THE PURPOSE

Is the purpose of your speech to persuade, inform, amuse? Unless you have a clear idea of your goal, you—and your speech —are apt to fizzle. So first of all, decide *what* you are trying to accomplish.

GATHER INFORMATION

Make sure it's authentic, up-to-date, and interesting. Read widely enough to get a "rounded" view of your topic, not just those sources that agree with your point of view. Put your information into a logical sequence in order to build toward the purpose you have in mind.

OUTLINE SPEECH

This needn't be a formal outline; just enough to indicate to yourself the progression of your thoughts (e.g., problem, causes, extent, cure). The point is, *get the broad sweep of your speech down on paper.*

PUT "MEAT" ON THE SKELETON

Once you have your outline, you are ready to beef it up with facts and figures. If, by their very nature, those facts are dry, make them more palatable by introducing them under the guise of examples, illustrations, or even an anecdote where suitable.

KEEP AUDIENCE IN MIND

Unless you "talk their language," your speech is apt to fall flat. What, generally, are they most interested in? If you keep this interest in mind and guide your speech-writing accordingly, you will almost surely come up with a winner.

MAKE SPEECH SOUND NATURAL

No speaker is invited to talk because he has an enormous vocabulary or expresses himself in interminably complex sentences. Remember, it is far more difficult to follow a line of thought by ear than by eye. What "reads" well does not necessarily "listen" well. So check your writing for *simplicity, brightness, good language,* and *accuracy.* Whenever in doubt about your choice of words, stick to the shorter one.

PRACTICE DELIVERY

If you speak too quickly or too slowly, you may be difficult to follow. Check your volume—few things are more irritating to an audience than a voice that can't always be heard. Get expression into your voice—a deadly monotone will alienate your listeners. Try not to have to read your speech verbatim; even if you fluff a line or two, your speech will have more impact if you look at your audience from time to time. If you have access to a tape recorder, tape your speech and listen to a playback as objectively as you can. If one isn't available, ask your wife for her criticism. And take it.

PRACTICAL SHORTHAND

If you've ever attended a meeting where the ideas flew thick and fast; or been on the telephone with somebody who threw a fistful of facts and figures at you faster than you could digest them; or been confronted with half a dozen pages of information to copy when your next appointment was just minutes away—then you are familiar with just a few of the many occasions that make an agile pencil literally worth its weight in diamonds.

Many business and professional men, discouraged by their

inability to take notes quickly, too often rely on memory. The results: embarrassing oversights, precious time wasted in backtracking, and costly errors.

To the rescue: a "quickie" training course in practical shorthand that can be mastered in minutes. There are just four rules.

1. ABBREVIATE

Almost every word in the English language can be shortened. Vowels in particular may be omitted. For example, "Satisfied customers have made our reputation" may be abbreviated, "Stsfd custs hv md r rep." With practice, you will find that it is easy to train your mind, and hand, to deal only with the skeletons of words.

2. OMIT UNESSENTIAL WORDS

It's seldom necessary to write down a word-for-word transcription of what you hear or read. Take the following excerpt:

> "I, for one, agree that the manufacturer's right arm is advertising in all its varied forms: newspapers, magazines, radio, television and direct mail."

None of the *meaning* is lost in this version, which is only one-third as long:

> "Mfr's rt arm is adv: paprs, mags, rad, TV & dir ml."

3. TAKE ADVANTAGE OF NATURAL ABBREVIATIONS

Look at the keys of any typewriter and you'll find a host of symbols that can help you cut your writing time: ¼, ½, # (number), %, $, ¢, @. Because of their pronunciation, certain letters and numbers may be substituted for common words: *b* (be), *r* (are, our), *u* (you), *y* (why), 2 (to, too), 4 (for). And don't overlook the convenience of such old stand-bys as

e. (that is), e.g. (for example), c (around, about, approximately).

Example: "Mr. Lewis is in Chicago and isn't expected back until about June tenth" becomes, "Lewis in Chi. Bck c. 6/10."

4. ADOPT A SYSTEM OF LETTERS FOR COMMON WORDS

Fewer than 100 words make up 50 percent of the average speaking vocabulary. If you can devise a system of letters for the most common words, you've licked half your problem. Many reporters use the following: f (from), w/ (with), w/o (without), xc (except), nst (instead), bc (because), h (he), w (we).

Example: "He failed because he thought only of himself. Without empathy, we are doomed." In "practical shorthand": "H faild bc h tht nly of hmsf. W/o mpthy, w r dmd."

With time, you can work out your own shorthand tricks, refining and improving on the methods described here. Try it! B4 u no it, ul be rtng fstr thn u evr tht psbl!

A SIMPLE WAY TO INCREASE
YOUR ABILITY TO CONCENTRATE

If you frequently find your mind wandering from what you *ought* to be doing, you probably can profit from the following exercise, first described by English psychologist A. R. Orage:

Take out your watch and observe the revolution of the second hand. It performs its circle in sixty seconds or one minute. Watch the hand as it begins a fresh circle and don't let your eye wander from it to the little dial; but keep your eye focused on the moving hand. When you are honestly certain that you can keep the focus of your attention on the moving hand for one revolution, you will have made an important step in the deliberate development of your ability to concentrate.

Now take another step. Keeping the focus as before, count mentally the numbers one to ten and backwards, slowly, during the course of one revolution of the hand. This requires a double attention, as it were. You are observing the movement and counting deliberately at the same time. At first, it may be easy, but do it again and again until it becomes difficult; and *then do it!* This is very important.

The next step is to add to these two simultaneous activities a third. While continuing to observe the moving hand with the eyes and counting with the mind, repeat to yourself some famous piece of verse; even a nursery rhyme will do.

The exercise can be made progressively difficult by adding fresh subjects for the attention. Two or three minutes at a time is enough.

Practice this often, whenever you have a spare minute and the effect on your ability to concentrate will speedily be marked.

NIPPING TENSION IN THE BUD

Lions and tigers, so far as we know, never get headaches. One reason is that they can growl. We civilized mortals usually bottle up our emotions, especially on the job. Result: unreleased tensions build up.

Usually, tension is localized in the neck, shoulders and back. The trick is to loosen your muscles in these areas before they become too tight.

Here are five easy actions you can take, even if you are desk-bound, to prevent tension from building:

1. Shrug your shoulders a few times after completing a regular action like signing a stack of letters, dictating, talking on the telephone for some time.
2. Take a deep breath every time you sit down.
3. Lean back and stretch hard at least once every half hour.
4. Place your hands on opposite sides of a doorway and push sideways every time you go through.
5. Bend down and touch your toes every time you get up from your chair. Let your arms and shoulders fall loose.

HOW TO WORK UNDER PRESSURE

With some justification, ours has been termed the Aspirin Age. We work under an assortment of pressures: time, money, the twin specters of failure and criticism, to name a few. Frequently, the sense of pressure builds up in the form of lack of self-confidence.

If you find yourself in a "pressure squeeze," try this program, designed to keep you working at peak performance.

First, identify the pressure. Until you know what you're fighting, you can't fight it effectively. It's the unknown that frightens us. Step one, therefore, is to pinpoint the kind of pressure you're up against. Is it a deadline? Fear of losing prestige? Doubts as to your ability? What? If necessary, take a few minutes and actually write out a short description of the "enemy."

Second, find out if it's real. Test it for authenticity. Is the pressure real or imaginary? Did someone actually name—or imply—it? Does it really exist? Are you sure? (Sometimes, the pressure under which we are working is self-inflicted.) Are you perhaps being too severe with yourself, demanding too much? If, upon examination, the pressure turns out to be real, take the next logical step.

This third step is to seek the antidote. Now is the time to ask yourself, "How can this pressure be reduced—or eliminated?" Try every possible answer. If, for example, the pressure is a limited amount of time in which to draw up a report, some possible antidotes might be: a) get an extension of time; b) get additional help; c) work two additional hours each night. Depending upon the feasibility of each alternative, you will, in time, eliminate two of the possibilities.

The final, logical step is to apply the antidote. The course of action dictated by the three preliminary steps may not always be easy or even pleasant. But if you follow the formula, you will have the satisfaction of knowing, at this point, that *you are doing what must be done;* and that you have arrived at the antidote through the use of every man's ultimate weapon, that is, his intelligence.

HOW TO IMPROVE YOUR VOICE

How you sound to others often determines their reactions to you as a person. A shrill, tense voice alienates; a pleasant, relaxed one attracts. Want an idea of how you sound to others? Use a tape recorder. If you don't have access to one, stand with your face about nine inches from a corner of a room, cup your ears with your hands and say something into the corner. What *you* hear is approximately what others do when you speak. Like it? Good! If you suspect that there might be room for improvement, however, try the following suggestions:

KEEP YOUR VOCAL CORDS RELAXED

Tenseness tightens vocal cords, thereby shortens them. Result: a higher pitch. Squeezing sounds through clenched teeth tenses your vocal cords—and your listener. So open your mouth and relax your jaw when you speak.

MOVE YOUR LIPS WHEN YOU TALK

If you don't give full value to vowels, your speech will sound slurred, be difficult to follow. Don't be afraid to pucker on sounds like "oo," as in *room* or *tool*. We rarely move our lips as much as we think we do. Practice before a mirror and you'll see.

DETERMINE THE BASIC PITCH OF YOUR VOICE

Monotony can be caused by tension or strain. Many of us speak several tones too high to begin with. By starting off too high, we have no place to go unless we strain some more. The solution is to discover your best basic pitch from which to raise or lower your tones. By trial and error, with hands cupping ears as you face a corner of a room, lower your pitch until it sounds soft and pleasant. *This is your basic pitch.* With it, you have room on your speech scale to raise an important word without forcing or to lower it for an interesting change of tone.

SUIT YOUR VOICE TO WHAT YOU'RE SAYING

If you've ever watched a hypnotist at work, you know his secret: a soothing monotone. Want to lull your listener to sleep? Then do the same thing. But if you want to create interest in what you are saying, develop vocal ups and downs, vary the pace of your speech, and let your voice reflect the meaning of key words. Thus, "That's the **best** idea I've **ever** heard!" leaves no doubt as to what you mean; you're using your voice as a true instrument of communication.

WHAT'S YOUR TIME WORTH?

Delegate a job; or add it to your own chores? Hire a painter; or "do-it-yourself"? Take that extra half-hour for lunch? Knock off early today? If you knew *exactly* how much your time was worth, you might find that such questions answer themselves. Based on 244 eight-hour working days a year, here is an eye-opening chart that will tell you the true value of your time. (You might want to show this to the people who work for you, too.)

If you earn	Every hour is worth	Every minute is worth	In a year, one hour a day is worth
$10,000	$ 5.12	.0852	$1250
12,000	6.15	.1025	1500
15,000	7.68	.1278	1875
20,000	10.25	.1708	2500
25,000	12.81	.2135	3125
35,000	17.93	.2988	4375
40,000	20.50	.3416	5000
50,000	25.61	.4269	6250

And, just in case . . .

$1,000,000	$512.30	$8.523	$125,000

DO YOU IRRITATE PEOPLE?

Many executives, who are acutely aware of the importance of good public relations at the corporate level, will think nothing of puffing cigar smoke into their secretaries' faces . . . speaking abruptly over the telephone to colleagues . . . keeping callers waiting unconscionably long in an anteroom.

Simple bad manners? Seldom.

Why, then, do they behave that way?

Because, over a period of time, they have permitted themselves to acquire a veneer of personal quirks, annoying mannerisms and bad habits that are anathema to others. As they rise in their companies, fewer and fewer people feel brave enough to tell them off. Eventually, these mannerisms ossify and become integral, and unattractive, parts of their overall personalities.

Ever suspect that you may be guilty?

To make sure that you aren't, here is a checklist of "little things" that frequently annoy people. Admittedly, none of these by itself may be serious. But in combination they could be hurting your own public relations and, consequently, your ability to work through and with others smoothly.

DO YOU WIN ARGUMENTS, BUT LOSE GOOD WILL?

Do you refuse to give ground gracefully even when you have been proved in error? Do you bring up subjects that easily become controversial on a personal level, like religion or politics? Do you find yourself "pulling rank" in disagreements with others?

DO YOU CALL OTHERS "STUPID"?

Not outrightly, of course, but it amounts to the same thing if you constantly say, "See what I mean?" or "You understand?" When you ask questions like these, you imply doubt in the other fellow's ability to follow you.

DO YOU PLAY FAVORITES?

There is no quicker road to sagging morale than to show favoritism in your day-to-day relationships. Granted, some employees *are* brighter, better looking, or more personally magnetic than others, but it's part of your job not to display personal bias, except as it relates to job performance. It is, for example, perfectly proper to assign a job to a man who is better equipped to handle it than another; it is improper to invite one particular employee to lunch day after day and to ignore his peers.

ARE YOU RUDE?

Do you interrupt others, cutting them off in the middle of a statement? Are you loud, bulling your way through an office and interfering with others' work? Rank has its privileges, to be sure, but they do not include raucous behavior.

DO YOU CRITICIZE OTHER DEPARTMENTS?

"Why don't you people wake up and come out of the Stone Age?" "You sure have a lot of red tape holding things up around here." A sure route to hard feelings is to heap scorn on another's area of responsibility. He may have devoted his entire working life to building up the department you're knocking. Even if he hasn't, nobody likes to hear disparaging remarks about something with which he is intimately connected.

DO YOU KILL IDEAS?

That is, if someone tries an idea out on you, do you usually pooh-pooh it simply because it challenges the status quo? Do you tend to judge the worth of an idea according to the title of the man propounding it? If an idea is obviously poor, do you enjoy bursting the originator's balloon? Or do you try to let him down with tact? A lot of managers discourage original thinking because they view any departure from "things-as-they-are" with abnormal suspicion.

DO YOU EMBARRASS OTHERS?

Some men forget that their secretaries are present when they lose their tempers. Others simply don't care who hears them give vent to their feelings. Still others appear to derive some bizarre satisfaction from taking out their frustrations on the nearest innocent. The momentary relief offered by some purple rhetoric is all too brief, however, and you have to face those you may have offended five days a week, week in and week out. So think twice before letting go.

DO YOU SEEK GLORY?

There is no surer way to murder initiative in others than to convince them that their contributions will never be recognized. Insist on taking all the credit for the accomplishments of those under you and you are apt to find your employee turnover increasing alarmingly.

DO YOU OVER-SUPERVISE?

Similarly, if you insist on keeping an eagle eye on every phase of every person's work, the obvious conclusion is that you trust no one's ability or judgment. If you delegate a job, by all means check on progress occasionally, but don't breathe down everybody's neck.

DO YOU LACK ENTHUSIASM?

That "blah" feeling can be highly contagious, and bored, uninspired subordinates seldom turn out more than routine work. If you are tired, ill, or not in the mood, you will do yourself and those under you a favor by making yourself scarce.

There you have them—ten "little things" that may be standing in the way of your success with others. If you suspect that any of these habits are sabotaging your own public relations, take counter-measures immediately. Grow purposefully self-conscious. Police yourself by watching how you behave in front of others and their reactions to you. Encourage your friends, family, and trusted colleagues to point out any annoying mannerisms you may possess. Accept their criticisms gracefully, work on them and you will stamp out the "executive gremlins" in your life.